Improving Student Behavior

What if you could use a handpicked set of tools to help children redirect their classroom behavior from dysfunctional to positive? *Improving Student Behavior: The Success Diary Approach* is a step-by-step guide to promoting your students' personal development. This book introduces The Success Diary, a novel, easy-to-use method for involving students in their own behavior modification plans. Designed by an experienced school psychologist, this guide consolidates approaches from various schools of behavioral intervention and integrates them into a streamlined, adaptable framework for teachers looking to engage with children's unique personalities, skills, motivations, and support systems to create lasting behavioral change. Through these flexible, common-sense guidelines and activities, you can empower your students to participate in working towards better behaviors and healthy social-emotional development.

Ami Braverman, Ph.D., is an experienced School Psychologist and Behavior Intervention Specialist. He is the creator of MaterialPsychology.com, a back-to-basics self-help toolbox for teachers.

Other Eye On Education Books Available from Routledge
(www.routledge.com/eyeoneducation)

**Differentiated Instruction Made Practical:
Engaging the Extremes through Classroom Routines**
Rhonda Bondie and Akane Zusho

**The Self-Regulated Learning Guide:
Teaching Students to Think in the Language of Strategies**
Timothy J. Cleary

**Five Teaching and Learning Myths—Debunked:
A Guide for Teachers**
Adam Brown and Althea Bauernschmidt

**The Passion-Driven Classroom:
A Framework for Teaching and Learning, 2nd Edition**
Angela Maiers and Amy Sandvold

**Universal Design for Learning in the Early Childhood Classroom:
Teaching Children of all Languages, Cultures, and Abilities, Birth – 8 Years**
Karen Nemeth and Pamela Brillante

**Stop, Think, Act:
Integrating Self-Regulation in the Early Childhood Classroom**
Megan M. McClelland and Shauna L. Tominey

**Inquiry and Innovation in the Classroom:
Using 20% Time, Genius Hour, and PBL to Drive Student Success**
A.J. Juliani

**Sticky Assessment:
Classroom Strategies to Amplify Student Learning**
Laura Greenstein

Improving Student Behavior

The Success Diary Approach

Ami Braverman

NEW YORK AND LONDON

First published 2019
by Routledge
52 Vanderbilt Avenue, New York, NY 10017

and by Routledge
2 Park Square, Milton Park, Abingdon, Oxon, OX14 4RN

Routledge is an imprint of the Taylor & Francis Group, an informa business

© 2019 Taylor & Francis

The right of Ami Braverman to be identified as author of this work has been asserted by him in accordance with sections 77 and 78 of the Copyright, Designs and Patents Act 1988.

All rights reserved. No part of this book may be reprinted or reproduced or utilised in any form or by any electronic, mechanical, or other means, now known or hereafter invented, including photocopying and recording, or in any information storage or retrieval system, without permission in writing from the publishers.

Trademark notice: Product or corporate names may be trademarks or registered trademarks, and are used only for identification and explanation without intent to infringe.

Library of Congress Cataloging-in-Publication Data
A catalog record for this title has been requested

ISBN: 978-1-138-36281-9 (hbk)
ISBN: 978-1-138-36282-6 (pbk)
ISBN: 978-0-429-77729-5 (ebk)

Typeset in Palatino
by Integra Software Services Pvt. Ltd.

Dedication

My dearest wife Esther, it is so commendable, your sincere devotion to our family's pursuit of meaningful dreams. We flourish.

Contents

List of Concept Boxes viii
Acknowledgments ix
Meet the Author x

   Introduction 1
1 Approaching Dysfunctional Behavior as a Team: Form a Collaborative Triangle 14
2 Agreeing on the Dysfunctional Behavior: Name the Problem 24
3 Consider the Cause of the Behavior: Postulate a Theory about the Motivation 30
4 Finding Alternatives to Dysfunctional Behavior: Define a Required Skill Set 41
5 Time to Address the Dysfunctional Behavior: Make a Success Diary 56
6 Improving Behavior: Encourage a Sense of Capability 63
7 Changing the Dysfunctional Behavior: Monitor for Success 73

Concept Boxes

0.1	Gestalt in the Classroom: The Power of the Day-to-Day	10
1.1	The Development of Personality through Parental Projection	19
1.2	Coping with Teachers' Guilt	20
2.1	Normalizing Problems	26
3.1	Functional Behavioral Assessments	31
3.2	Recognizing an Unmotivated Child	33
4.1	Re-framing and Saying "No" with a Smile	43
4.2	The Parameters of a Self-sustaining Transformation	53
5.1	The Mindfulness Bottle	61
6.1	Forming Positive Memories of a Skill Set	65
7.1	Material Psychology	77
7.2	Reinforcing a Learning Experience	80

Acknowledgments

I will always say that my job is to sell people things they already own. To every teacher that I have worked with and learned from, every educator out there, thank you for what you do. You are doing a crucial job. This book is a guide for what you already own: ingenuity, care, and strength.

Prof. Joseph Tzelgov, you taught me the nature of opinion. Even the smartest theories can be questioned and this is a comforting thought. One does not have to be Einstein to have a valid opinion, since everyone can be wrong!

Udi Beck and Lika Hatzir, you have both taught me how to inject personality into my work. Udi, you use your charisma as a therapeutic tool in a manner that I aspire to. Lika, your guidance showed me that it is possible to be both positive and pragmatic in my clinical approach.

And lastly, I would like to thank my mother, Ella. Your feedback and support helped me set the stage.

Meet the Authors

Ami Braverman, Ph.D., is an experienced researcher, School Psychologist, and Behavior intervention Specialist. A born writer, he owned a typewriter before he learned to ride a bicycle, composing existential poems at age 10.

He began his professional career working for seven years in an experimental psychology laboratory, researching executive functioning, decision making, and memory. He subsequently earned an M.A. and a Ph.D. in Cognitive Psychology and has published articles in prestigious journals such as Brain & Cognition. Seeking a more hands-on career he then began working as a School Psychologist in multiple schools, ages pre K-12. He describes the transition into the school setting as a feeling of coming-home. Ever since, he has been dedicated in his pursuit to assist families and teachers in their personal development. A true believer in inventive self-actualization, he is the creator of MaterialPsychology.com, a back-to-basics self-help toolbox for teachers.

Introduction

Modifying Dysfunctional Behaviors: Injecting Personality into the Intervention

If you are reading this book, you are probably searching for a new approach to dealing with a child that has troubling behaviors. Being a teacher yourself, you are well aware that people in this profession are required to face much more than one would initially assume.

You could be trying to lower disruptions during lessons or stop fights during breaks.

Or you could be attempting to encourage an unmotivated child to study more, to learn new habits, or to persevere with character-building activities.

Maybe you are endeavoring to prevent a student from leaving the classroom without permission or are engaged in motivating a troubled adolescent in choosing not to quit school.

If you are a veteran teacher, I am sure that you have encountered bizarre situations, such as looking for ways to encourage a child to take regular baths, counseling a child on the reasons why not to sniff aerosol, stopping a boy from selling haircuts in the bathroom, or encountering a group responsible for graffiti in the school.

These are only a few examples of child behaviors that are maladaptive or dysfunctional. Maladaptive because they cause the children to stand out in a negative way, making integrating into society harder for them; dysfunctional because they seemingly are motivated by a need for disruption and not growth.

A child presenting with dysfunctional behavior not only poses challenges to your ability to educate him/her, but can also disrupt the ability of other children in the classroom to take part in a lesson.

And truthfully, children are not the only difficulty that you as a teacher face when it comes to dysfunctional behavior.

Even teachers new to the job can attest to the varying obstacles that they encounter when trying to collaborate with parents on child education (emotional, social, and academic). I mention this not as a rebuke towards parents but rather as an understanding of the various trials that teachers go through in order to manage child behavior. Notice that I do not mention the stress that administration can pose on teachers (they may also be reading this book).

Needless to say, dysfunctional child behavior can put an enormous strain on everyone involved, including other children, teachers, parents, administration, and social services.

In fact, it is such a commonplace phenomenon that a multitude of methods to address this problem have been developed throughout the years (and continue to be developed). These derive from a number of therapeutic approaches, including Applied Behavior Analysis, Cognitive Behavioral Therapy, and Psychodynamic Theory. The techniques developed are sometimes general (e.g. class-wide token systems) and other times specific (i.e. to an individual diagnosis or type of behavior).

In other words, you are not alone. Everybody is wondering what to do.

Honestly, with so many cooks in the kitchen it can get quite confusing when approaching particular scenarios, especially since the differing theories are founded on principles that often seemingly conflict. For example, an applied behavior analyst would not be very interested in past conflicts but rather focus on current behaviors, whereas a psychodynamic analyst would focus on resolving past conflicts, especially from early upbringing, and see current behaviors simply as symptoms.

To add on to this, the wealth of resources illustrating and delineating the numerous techniques are usually not easily approachable for teachers, since the various methods and jargon are generally developed for mental health professionals such as applied behavior analysts, psychologists, social workers, counselors, and so on.

Not to worry. You are not alone. This book was developed specifically for teachers.

My goal is to provide you with a down-to-earth guide to dysfunctional behaviors, a handpicked set of the tools that my mentors, my colleagues, and I myself have found most useful. Each one is like that screwdriver that can get the most stubborn screw out, attach a picture frame to concrete, hammer in nails, open up a stubborn pickle jar, and even reach that hard-to-reach spot on your back that needs a scratch. Some of the tools are just useful ways of looking at a problem, whereas others are practical steps towards a solution.

In other words, *Improving Student Behavior: The Success Diary Approach* is a conspectus of techniques and clinical concepts, from multiple perspectives, for teachers dealing with dysfunctional child behavior.

It is a multi-tiered, step-by-step approach that culminates in the development and utilization of an individualized Success Diary. Each one of these steps and guidelines alone may prove sufficient in redirecting a child to more functional behavior. The more complex scenarios would require most or all steps, including making and using a unique behavioral intervention, The Success Diary.

The distinctive aspect of this approach is the minimalistic integration between various psychological and educational methods.

Having first spent seven years of my career in an experimental psychology laboratory, and then making a less common transition into the more clinical fields of school psychology and behavior intervention, I have been afforded multiple diverse perspectives. Leaning on various findings/models of cognitive psychology (the foundation for Applied Behavioral methods and Cognitive Behavioral Therapy), I have been able to base my therapeutic interventions on well-known theories of emotion, development, behavior, learning, perception, and complex thinking. On the other hand, the clinical practices utilized by school psychologists and other clinicians have provided me with valuable tools in my quest to encourage meaningful change in people's lives. Combining these diverse perspectives has culminated in the development of this guide.

By bringing together these sometimes opposing bodies of work, it is possible to take the best of each world. Cognitive and Behavioral methods provide an effective, systematic approach to dealing with dysfunctional behavior. On the other hand, these can be quite demanding techniques, which require a specialist focusing on one specific child at a time, sometimes for extended periods of the day. This can be too cumbersome for one teacher that has a whole classroom of children to monitor. The integration of a few basic clinical precepts injects into these methods a much-needed element of flexibility and an emphasis on personality development.

The outcome is a tried and tested approach that has routinely resulted in a meaningful transformation in children previously presenting with dysfunctional behavior, not to mention an approach that is generally less demanding on the teacher and the child than are the majority of behavioral intervention plans.

My personal experience has also been a crucial resource for the development of this guide since I feel that only through direct work with children, parents, and teachers can one design a practical technique. This is the critical bridge between theory and practice. I have worked with clinicians, educators, parents, and children coming from diverse socioeconomic backgrounds and presenting with a plethora of problems. This, I hope, has allowed me to make the passages in this book as approachable as possible to a wide variety of teachers, out in the field.

Child behavior is a complicated subject with no quick fixes and there is no reason to make things more complex than they need to be.

I personally believe that utilizing examples is the best way to make theory more relatable and thus more approachable. So with no further ado, I would like to bring you an example from the very beginnings of my career, an experience that signaled to me what the principle message of my work, and this guide, needs to be. That is, children should, when possible, be an active part of their own treatment plan.

On my very first day of working at a school, I found myself drawn into a heated discussion between a teacher and a single father. This parent had a habit of taking his 9-year-old son with him to the beach where he played cards and smoked medical marijuana with other adults. The boy's teacher could not understand why the father was incapable of comprehending that this was unacceptable behavior.

As a school psychologist, fresh out of the box, I was highly motivated to succeed and promptly attempted to de-escalate the situation. I got both parties to calm down and to try to understand each other's viewpoint.

The father started to see the educational repercussions of these excursions to the beach, and the teacher began to see the emotional perspective of a confused and lonely single father with an undisclosed disability. The two then tailored a plan for future communication where the teacher could smoothly assist the father with these kinds of dilemmas and the father could try to be more open to her guidance.

Walking home that day, feeling smug about my great success, I received a phone call from the school counselor. The boy in question had been involved in a serious fight with a schoolmate and had been suspended.

I realized that my intervention was missing the most important cog in the therapeutic machine – involvement of the child. I had never met the boy. I could not even easily recall his name!

The truce I had brokered really was a success, a stepping-stone towards a therapeutic treatment plan. The boy, however, was unaware of our progress, and was still having behavioral and emotional problems.

We had not made him a part of his own therapeutic process, or made any plans to do so in the future. Why had he not been invited to that discussion or at least to a follow-up meeting? We had never even asked him what he felt he benefited from going to the beach with his father.

In other words, we wanted the boy to stop fighting in school but what did the boy want? Did he even feel capable of not fighting? Was he aware of better ways to resolve conflict?

Yes, there was now a better collaboration between father and teacher but this was very far from a comprehensive plan of action that enlisted the child into a therapeutic process.

You will see that at times collaboration between teachers and parents is enough for an intervention to succeed but, more often than not, I have witnessed that when it comes to dysfunctional behavior, a more thorough plan of action is required that includes the effective and affective participation of the child.

As I have observed throughout my career, too often children are not actively included in the therapeutic process. The child presents with disruptive behavior, a meeting is held to which the boy or girl is not invited, a course of action is decided upon, and the child is expected to comply and present us with positive results.

This is not to say that such treatment plans lack positive intent or intelligent design. Neither is it to say that we should not have expectations of a child; we most definitely should. It is more a question of the level of personal engagement. If someone willingly takes part in their individual treatment plan, they will potentially be more motivated to succeed, and will probably adopt a more personalized course of action. In other words, we want them to feel that their success is their own.

This in turn potentially triggers a more self-sustaining and therapeutic outcome. Think about it. If you knew that you had overcome an obstacle using a self-devised plan of action, would you not be more likely to use that strategy again? Even if you had been given assistance along the way, you would still value the outcome as something of your own volition, would you not?

Courses of action to address dysfunctional behavior modification not only need to be individualized, they need to feel personal.

In other words, aspects of personality need to be injected into behavior modification.

As you read on I hope that you will see the relevance of this statement.

The chapters in this book are written as a consecutive set of guiding stages for effective clinical/educational interventions for children, K-12, displaying dysfunctional behavior, which culminates in the implementation of a Success Diary.

The technique is geared towards teachers but has also been utilized by parents, counselors, school psychologists, and other professionals.

Allow me three side notes before carrying on with a description of the chapters. Firstly, a few case studies have been depicted in the pages of this book. Some alterations, such as the use of pseudonyms, have been used in order to maintain anonymity and confidentiality. The case studies that were selected generally relay quite common scenarios.

Secondly, this book in no way is intended to replace therapy or any other form of clinical intervention. Clinical terms such as treatment plan are utilized; however, this is not meant as a way to encourage teachers to provide treatment. This guide is a supplement for teachers who are already required to intervene with dysfunctional behaviors. Think of a Success Diary not as a behavior support plan that only certified professionals can implement but rather as a personalized behavior modification chart provided to you with a conspectus of tools to support your decision-making. Please ensure to follow laws and regulations regarding what is considered treatment and out of your scope (i.e. anything other than education) and use sound judgment (e.g. stop the intervention and get help if someone is being emotionally/physically harmed or is in danger of the same). It is recommended to work in tandem with a psychologist, school counselor, or social worker, in order to ensure that appropriate therapeutic tools are being utilized (e.g. children are referred to therapy or social services when needed).

Thirdly, I have made an effort to make the guide as readable and usable as possible. With that said, throughout the book you will encounter some professional terminology. Do not worry. About half of these terms are already mentioned in this introduction and will be expanded on further, in the following chapters.

Chapter 1 will focus on the importance of cultivating the developmental environment by consolidating a child's pre-existing support systems (i.e. school and home). When parents and teachers (or other professionals) work together, it decidedly raises the chances of truly engaging a child in their own therapeutic plan. In the absence of such collaboration, the school professionals, or parents, can still successfully implement a Success Diary by themselves. They will just need to put in extra effort in order to ensure that they are providing a communicative and motivating environment.

Chapter 2 elaborates on the subject of teamwork by giving this support team their first task, clearly defining the problem. Accomplishing this often-overlooked milestone is a sure sign that a productive collaboration has been achieved. Furthermore, by focusing on defining a problem prior to focusing on a solution, the team minimizes potential disagreements as it neutralizes premature discussion of solutions, which could potentially lead to conflicts.

In Chapter 3, the team works together to postulate a theory regarding the function of the child's behavior. As you will see, by knowing the motivation for the behavior the team can often already find a solution. The first strategy to finding this out is simply asking the child why he/she is behaving in a certain way. This is the first step towards putting accountability in the right hands (i.e. the child). In the end, it will always be the child's own responsibility to modify his/her behavior, no matter how much support the team provides.

Following this, in Chapter 4, if a resolution has not yet been achieved, the team will define a skill set that the child needs to work on. This stage, an integration of Cognitive Behavioral elements into Applied Behavioral methods, is possibly the most complex phase of the intervention. On the bright side, a well-defined skill set distinctly widens the chances of a positive outcome.

Chapter 5 consists of step-by-step instructions for preparing a Success Diary, the most important step being letting the child go through the process of taking ownership of their Success Diary through the use of creativity. This is the richest element of the technique in regards to Psychodynamic Theory (i.e. directly related to personality).

You may be tempted to flip forward to this section in order to promptly learn the exact details of this behavioral intervention. My suggestion is to follow the flow of the book. There are many prerequisites to review that will enrich your understanding of the details. I can, however tell you that the tables once prepared are user-friendly and a minimal strain on you, the teacher. They do not look that dissimilar to the various behavior modification charts that you are probably already familiar with.

In Chapter 6, I elaborate on the key concept behind The Success Diary; with this tool you can assist a child in gaining a sense of capability. My doctrine is that most cases of children (and often adults) presenting with dysfunctional behaviors occur when a child feels incapable of reaching his/her goals in a more functional manner. By emphasizing a sense of capability you, the teacher, can address dysfunctional behavior in a highly empowering and empathetic style encouraging healthy social and emotional development.

Chapter 7 is a practical guide on how to use The Success Diary, once it has been made. The technique is a positively focused one, so the emphasis is on monitoring for level of success and keeping the child motivated. This chapter includes a summary of everything covered.

Throughout this book you will encounter supplementary concept boxes that enrich the content with personal side notes and academic theory. It is not necessary to follow these in order to utilize the guide or implement a Success Diary. With that said, these boxes describe significant supportive information that may prove useful to any teacher dealing with dysfunctional behavior.

It is important to indicate that the collection of ideas and tools described throughout this book are my own viewpoint, based on cognitive research, clinical theories, frequently used techniques, my personal and professional experience, as well as what I hope is a large dose of common sense. I have not invented the wheel; just put a list of prevailing concepts and approaches together in a way that I hope will be useful to you, the teacher. Some elements of the guide are a bit more complex, whereas others are so simple as to seem obvious. The latter, however, should not be overlooked. I believe that recognizing the obvious can often lead to positive and potent outcomes. This sentiment is familiar to many different schools of thought.

On a final note, before we begin, The Success Diary is not just about injecting a child's personality into his/her own therapeutic plan; it is also about you injecting your personality into the process. As you read this book, I invite you to form your own opinions, based on your individual viewpoint, and thus to expand on your personal skill set.

I truly believe that everyone in their own right is a researcher of psychology and human behavior from their personal and unique perspective. Laws, educational perspectives, therapeutic methods, these all vary over time but you will always remain the professional. You may not be providing children with formal therapy, yet by being a teacher (or a parent) you are already providing a developmental environment (refer to Concept Box 0.1 for an elaboration on this). The concepts and methods relayed in this book ought to be viewed as tools for tweaking this pre-existing environment.

CONCEPT BOX #0.1

Gestalt in the Classroom: The Power of the Day-to-Day

Before making a decision to do more for a child, it is always advised to review everything that you, the teacher, are already undertaking. This is important since what you are doing on a daily basis has power that should not be underestimated.

Teachers take upon themselves a sizable amount of tasks (as well as a bunch more that are thrust upon them). I have discovered, however, that if asked to write a comprehensive list of these undertakings, they are usually stumped. Try it. Take a piece of paper and start writing what you already do for the child in question. You will start off slowly but before you know it, you will see that one page is not enough.

Here is a short sample list of some things that you probably do:

1. teach
2. come to work on time
3. take attendance
4. prepare supplies
5. organize the classroom
6. decorate the classroom
7. collaborate with parents
8. give homework
9. check homework
10. put together tests
11. check tests
12. break up arguments
13. manage dysfunctional behavior
14. communicate with the principal
15. assist children with social issues
16. relay worrying information (e.g. potential neglect) to child services
17. assist in making and following through with individualized education plans for children with learning disabilities
18. continue your own education (e.g. reading this book)
19. accompany children on school outings
20. participate/organize school festivities.

The response I have received from every single teacher, after completing this exercise, has invariably been the same. These are considered obvious duties that are just part of the job and they want to know what they need to do for a specific child.

But these regular, day-to-day tasks are a major element of the developmental environment that you are providing for the child. The fact that they are obvious does not mean that they are not powerful.

In many ways, the opposite is true. Ask anyone that suddenly went from knowing that supper is a daily occurrence to an existence where steady meals are hard to come by. They will tell you how potent a phenomenon an obvious daily supper can be. It is an archetypal symbol of a maintained household.

Let us look at an example from your classroom. What would happen to the children in your class if you did not check their homework? Well, first of all, most of them would try to get away with not doing homework.

More importantly, though, is the fact that the children would not be given the opportunity to work on the skill of doing homework. In turn, this could affect their ability to acquire functional habits towards self-reliance.

In short, any act that engenders an environment that encourages development is therapeutic.

Yes, checking homework is therapeutic.

In psychology this is referred to as gestalt – the value of all of your actions are higher than the sum of them together. The act of checking homework on a daily basis, for a full year, equals more than just the cumulative time taken to check the homework.

The worth of the day-to-day is higher than what it may feel like on a single day but the unwavering repetition of this action is what gives it its power.

This is just one example of stable practices that you maintain in your classroom. There are many more. Look at the list of things that you already do for a child in question. How many of these provide a developmental environment?

This stability that you already provide is a cornerstone of healthy child development. It is a potent tool in gaining vital behavioral and emotional habits. Any new behavioral intervention should be viewed as supplemental to what you are already providing. You already do a lot!

Another advantage of understanding the power of the day-to-day is that you, as the teacher, are often in the most viable position to implement a behavioral intervention that requires consistent monitoring, such as The Success Diary.

> Following the same logic of checking homework every day, can you imagine the potential effect you can have on a child with dysfunctional behavior? For example, a boy that needs to learn to stop pulling girls' hair could easily be influenced by daily reminders to treat girls with more respect. This alone can often be sufficient in directing a child towards more functional behavior.

The Success Diary works because it calls upon you to use your intuition. Your behavioral interventions depend on how sure you feel about your own abilities. I have met many teachers and I can tell you without ever meeting you, you are already capable!

1

Approaching Dysfunctional Behavior as a Team

Form a Collaborative Triangle

As mentioned in the Introduction, when trying to modify dysfunctional behavior, all-around cooperation and communication is of the utmost importance. In therapeutic and educational situations, it is common practice to utilize the triangle analogy. In this case, the triangle consists of the parents in one corner, you, the teacher in the second corner, and the child in the third corner. The last component is obviously the most important since without a child's active participation, even the best therapeutic treatment plan has little chance of success. With that said, optimally, prior to enlisting a child into an intervention, parents and teachers need to form a smooth collaboration. This in turn assists in establishing a healthy, unequivocal message for the child.

Making Expectations Clear to the Child by Working as a Team

Giving clear and consistent signals as to what is required of children is an environmental factor, critical to healthy functioning and development.

In my experience, most teachers have good ideas on how to communicate expectations of a child. Parents too, regarding establishing this at home.

A common problem is that the two parties often have differing ideas on what the message needs to be. That is not to say that one approach is necessarily better than the other, just different. However, when parents and teachers are not on the same page, they may often convey an inconsistent message to a child, regarding what is expected of him/her.

By working together, by forming two corners of the collaborative triangle, parents and teachers take a definitive step toward stabilizing a child's developmental environment by making expectations clear.

Children Naturally Want to Behave Functionally

I believe that most children have an innate desire to please and to do what they believe is expected of them as signaled by their environment.

Children look to their surroundings for cues on how to act. They try to adapt to their environment as a way of attaining personal desires (e.g. getting food; getting play; getting attention). Preferably this is achieved in a functional manner (i.e. without negative consequences to self or others); however, if it is not clear to the child how to do so, then he/she could potentially utilize a dysfunctional behavior instead.

The goal of forming a collaborative triangle is to develop a climate optimized at allowing children to act on their natural motivation to behave in a functional manner. In other words, make it clear to the child functional ways of adapting to the environment.

Parent–Teacher Collaboration Can Alone Phase Out Dysfunctional Behavior

The following case study illustrates the utility of positive communication between parents and the teacher. Joseph, an

8-year-old boy, presented as hyperactive and uncommunicative. He would engage in self-gratifying behaviors with very little connection to what was expected of him during the lesson, often getting up and walking to other tables. This seemingly random behavior disrupted his own ability to learn as well as that of other students.

In her attempts to stop him from disturbing the lesson, his teacher would often encounter acute resistance on his part, which included hitting other students, running out of the classroom, and throwing stones at kindergartners.

On a few occasions, I witnessed Joseph having what appeared to be a psychotic episode. For extended periods, he would regress into dysfunctional play, pretending that he was a dinosaur, "forgetting" how to speak, and hitting imaginary characters and even himself with a stick.

To complicate matters, the school counselor brought to my attention that a few months earlier, Joseph had been involved in a traumatic experience. He had been alone in his family home and allegedly set fire to the kitchen. Apparently, his parents could not watch him after school since they both worked late.

This was a disturbing case that raised multiple red flags.

I requested a team meeting with the parents and the school professionals. What came across during this meeting was a complete inability of the parties to find a middle ground.

Joseph's teacher was worried about his hyperactive behavior and wanted him to be "put on medication."

His principal wondered if the school was a good fit.

The school counselor wanted him to get treatment for a clear-cut case of PTSD.

His parents absolutely refused to see that Joseph had any problems while blaming the teacher for not doing enough.

Every person had a point to make and no one was willing to compromise.

I needed to find a way to assist the team in collaborating. It dawned on me that everyone in the room came from a different cultural background, so I changed the topic of the conversation to cultural differences in childrearing. As the conversation progressed, the cultural differences became more and more apparent.

It was easy to see how Joseph could be confused as to the behavioral expectations placed upon him.

The teacher had come from a religious home, believing in the importance of structured surroundings.

The principal grew up in a big city, a true believer in the importance of strengthening individuality.

The counselor was from a farming town and stated that a strong social environment is the most important part of development.

Most importantly, the parents were immigrants from a country where admitting to emotional maladies was a taboo. Having any disability, especially an emotional one, was unacceptable since it would be seen as an attempt to evade work. Becoming a productive part of society was a "normal" expectation and anyone that did not conform was ostracized.

This act of personal sharing had an immediate effect. The unmentionable elephant in the room of cultural differences became less of a barrier to all and once it was out in the open, the different parties were better able to communicate.

They understood a bit more where every person was coming from and thus found it easier to approach each other.

We could now focus on cooperation, putting Joseph in the focal point, instead of the personal differences between the parties involved. The team set up a clear schedule for phone conversations and developed a teacher–parent communication logbook. This log would assist in holding Joseph accountable for his behavior, as well as relaying a united front. The unequivocal message was that Joseph was expected to follow the teacher's directives in the classroom.

I do not think that this had previously been apparent to him.

Within less than a month, an improvement in Joseph's behavior and emotional state was more than evident. He was communicative, social, and attempting to catch up academically. I observed this transformation in even the smallest details of his day. Joseph spent more time playing with other children and he had clearly become more comfortable with his teacher, communicating to her when something was bothering him, instead of having a tantrum.

The mixed signals this boy had been getting from his extended environment had been replaced with a clear and consistent message from all fronts. Thus, the various expectations of him had become illuminated. This alone had proven sufficient in motivating him to behave in a more functional manner.

As mentioned in the Introduction, the principal message of this guide is that children need to actively participate in the various phases of their personal therapeutic plan. With that said, as can be seen, this first step of forming a collaborative triangle, starting with the two "corners" of teacher and parents, can at times be sufficient in changing the dysfunctional behavior.

Collaborating with parents is a learned skill

Of course, achieving this collaboration with parents and maintaining it is a team effort not dependent on you alone. Many veteran teachers that I have worked with have also mentioned that working with parents is a skill that requires practice.

Every educator approaches this task differently. Focusing on cultural differences is only one path. Some teachers like to make things personal, whereas others prefer to maintain an aura of professionalism. Some actively reach out to parents on a steady basis, whereas others simply establish an open door policy.

A good way of conceptualizing this task of collaborating with parents is that you, as the teacher, have an expectation of forming an alliance with the parents, to the level that they are willing. This is not done forcefully but yes, consistently. As I like to say, "the door is always open." Refer to Concept Boxes 1.1 and 1.2 where I explore two possible hindrances to teacher's being able to collaborate with parents.

CONCEPT BOX #1.1

The Development of Personality through Parental Projection

At times, enlisting the parents into a therapeutic plan can be a daunting task. Parents often show resistance that seems to defy logic. For example, it is not uncommon to find parents who claim that their illiterate teenage son or daughter does not have an academic problem. Often these parents are actually quite involved and obviously caring but may also be defensive, adopting the countenance of "us against them."

Why are they opposing the system so hard, especially when it can become detrimental to the development of their own child? I believe these parents are doing something natural. They are fighting for their child's personality, whether real or imagined.

A child's personality begins in the mind of the parents. Even prior to conception, parents already envision who their baby will become. As their child is born and grows, parents project onto their child an image of who they want him or her to develop into.

This process begins with only snippets of character and moves on to a full-blown personality. They have hopes and dreams for the person that is coming into being, expectations that play a pivotal role in development. The parents are going through the healthy mechanism of guiding their children towards a balanced personality.

Children are initially predisposed to adapt to the parental expectations of who they need to be but as they progress through the various stages of development a natural element of rebellion arises. The child must learn to define his/her own personality. In other words, as time passes and their child grows, the parents are required to go through the complex process of letting go.

Many parents have difficulties with this, especially if they are required to accept negative aspect of their child.

The case study of Joseph is a good example of this. His parents were projecting on him a much-revered characteristic of learning to be a hard worker. His dysfunctional behavior was seemingly in contradiction with this sentiment, especially taking cultural factors into consideration. Theoretically, this could be reason enough for the parents denying the obvious behavioral concerns.

You as the teacher at times are put in a position where you are relaying to a parent that their child is not who they think they are. This can be an unpleasant situation to be in but it is important to try to adapt to the parents' pace with regards to accepting the problem. This may cause a delay in the therapeutic plan but it is a very worthwhile delay if the outcome is the culmination of the aforementioned developmental milestone, laying down the foundations for the development of a balanced personality.

Unfortunately, not all parents succeed in completing this process in a timely fashion and in the more extreme cases, where neglect seems evident, social services needs to be notified. Of course, every situation should be evaluated separately.

CONCEPT BOX #1.2

Coping with Teachers' Guilt

Working with parents can at times be a daunting task but, truthfully, not only parents are resistant to collaboration. Sometimes teachers too can come across as opposing to a therapeutic plan. A common cause for this is teacher's guilt.

As a teacher you are exposed to children in hardship and sometimes even in dire straits. Some children are having various academic difficulties, while others are developing deep emotional issues.

This exposure comes with a price tag.

Teachers experience a natural urge to "fix" the children's problems and to steer them clear of oncoming, perceived disasters. Since this often is impossible, teachers habitually feel frustrated and, yes, even guilty.

Some teachers react to this feeling of guilt by becoming desensitized and may therefore come across as passive or uncaring.

Others become hypersensitive and feel the urge to do, often much more than they are expected to.

It is also not uncommon for teacher's guilt to contribute to negative self-perceptions. There may be a sense of inadequacy on the job, something that can cause a teacher at times to be quite defensive.

There is no clear-cut way of treating teacher's guilt since everyone manages it in a different way; however, I have found that it is important to be aware of the phenomenon when working in an educational institution.

The guilt does not disappear; rather, it is a stressor of the job that professionals need to learn to adapt to. I know that I have felt it many a time. Having an awareness of the matter is the first step towards developing this skill. Some jobs require people to wear hard hats; education jobs require people to consistently work on personal emotional resilience.

If you find yourself having difficulties coping with teacher's guilt (e.g. ruminating about children after work, snapping at parents, feeling overly anxious before lessons), I suggest speaking to your school psychologists or other supports that you have been provided with. I myself have assisted a number of teachers on their journey to becoming more resilient in the face of the potential and often inevitable guilt that accompanies the educational profession.

I wholeheartedly suggest leaning on your educational supports for advice (e.g. counselors, principals, school psychologists, other teachers) when encountering unique resistance from parents, especially since your colleagues may have tools to assist in the more challenging cases. For example, Joseph's school counselor consequently enrolled him in a subsidized after-school program so that he would not have to go home to an empty house. This was a factor that most probably assisted in stabilizing his developmental environment.

When Parents and Teachers are on the Same Page Children Feel Heard

Another aspect of maintaining a smooth collaboration with parents is that children may be more comfortable to communicate distress and/or any potential obstacles to functional behavior. Contrarily, if a child does not feel heard then he/she may escalate the message he/she is attempting to relay.

Dysfunctional behaviors can be seen as an extreme form of communication.

Think about yourself in an argument. If you feel that the other party is not listening to your side, what do you do? Most people will more strongly emphasize their point (e.g. exaggerate; make a harsh statement; raise their voices; walk away dramatically; finish the last popsicle in the freezer).

Using the same logic, if a child is signaling a need for something and no one responds, what might he/she do? Many will emphasize their point (e.g. run out of the classroom; hit other children; have a tantrum).

By catching distress signals in time, you can avoid the escalation of dysfunctional behaviors.

In short, the initial scope of the collaborative triangle is what is being communicated and what is being heard. Remember, feeling that he/she is being heard means that the child does not experience the urge to escalate. This in turn means that the child will be more available to listening when being educated/redirected.

Enlisting a Child into a Collaborative Triangle

As mentioned, without a child's active participation, even the best therapeutic treatment plan has little chance of success.

The goal is to enlist the child into the collaborative triangle, building trust.

This is more easily done once you and the parents have succeeded in forming the first two corners of the collaborative triangle. If you feel comfortable with the level of communication and mutual respect that you have with parents, you can suggest a meeting with the family as a whole.

Initially, it would be better not to focus on dysfunctional behaviors. The child should optimally not immediately associate meeting together with being in trouble. You can get together to discuss a child's personal dreams, hobbies, holiday experiences, etc. The subject matter can be anything you want. Just try to keep it positive. Remember, the first step is building a team with a high level of comfortable communication.

Homework for the Teacher

1. Identify everyone that is in your support system. Just knowing the people you can reach out to for advice/assistance can be a comfort.
2. Select parents that you feel you have formed an alliance with and try to determine how this success was achieved. What was your contribution to the positive collaboration and what was theirs?
3. Name one child in your classroom that possibly could be confused by divergent educational approaches between you and his/her parents.

2

Agreeing on the Dysfunctional Behavior

Name the Problem

In Chapter 1, I deliberated over the importance of forming a collaborative triangle. Now we can discuss the dysfunctional behavior, which needs to be investigated and defined. I call this stage "naming the problem," something that at first may seem straightforward. However, based on my experience, the team members tend to rush over this step towards various possible solutions, which in turn leads to resistance and elevated emotions, from all corners of the triangle. Focusing back on naming the problem often resolves these problems.

Prematurely Focusing on Solutions can be Counterproductive

I will continue with the case study of Joseph in order to elaborate on this point. A few months after the positive initial intervention, I met with Joseph's teacher and parents as a follow up. At first, his parents were very friendly, even bringing the teacher some home-baked bread. However, once she mentioned Joseph's continuing academic difficulties they became aggressive.

Joseph was not focused in lessons and he still could not read. The parents blamed the teacher for not giving Joseph enough attention. The teacher in turn became defensive, saying that the parents could not blame her since they refused to put him on medication for attention deficit disorder. As is often the case when two parties each feel that they are not being heard, they both gradually started raising voices.

I intervened by asking the simple question, "Can you name Joseph's problem?"

I pointed out to them that receiving more attention or being put on medication may or may not be possible solutions to a yet unnamed problem. Of course, everyone continued to argue, ignoring my point. Joseph's parents reiterated that they refused to put Joseph on medication and began to raise their voices towards me as well.

Dealing with Resistance to Naming the Problem

As you can see, when working towards naming a problem, heightened emotions may rise to the surface, so it is advisable to come with a bucket full of patience to these meetings. It is often the case that varying issues need to be resolved before the team is able to unanimously give a name to the problem.

Due to the severity of the parent's emotional response, I realized that we were not yet ready as a team to name the problem. I tried to lower the resistance by explaining that although taking these types of medications often leads to amazing therapeutic results, attention deficit disorder is not the only possible cause for academic difficulties. Furthermore, not everyone with such disorders is prescribed psychotropic medications. I also made it clear that many other parents were dealing with similar problems and many children have difficulties studying. This last technique is referred to as Normalization (refer to Concept Box 2.1).

> **CONCEPT BOX #2.1**
>
> **Normalizing Problems**
>
> Although crisis intervention is beyond the scope of this book, I have found two significant parallels between dealing with crisis situations and coming to terms with problems in a child. Firstly, parents need to come to a level of acceptance and, secondly, that doing so is a process, individual to every person. For this reason, in my eyes, it is important to be aware of one very useful tool utilized by mental health professionals during crisis intervention: Normalization.
>
> In short, Normalization is the process of moving phenomena perceived as extreme and usually aversive, into the realm of the norm. For example, parents dealing with a child that has been diagnosed with dyslexia may believe that their world is collapsing. It is therefore important to normalize by communicating to them that dyslexia is a common learning disability and that many children have learning disabilities. This is especially helpful if there is clear evidence that although a malady in question is an unpleasant obstacle, it is not something impossible to overcome. The object is to comfort the person and to show them that their world, though shaken, is not collapsing and with help, they can deal with it.
>
> A note of warning: Normalization is a complex technique used by professionals, often for traumatic situations, such as dealing with an attempted suicide. For this reason, one should tread very carefully when approaching parents with the intention of using this technique. Consider whether it would be better for a trained professional to deal with the situation.

Joseph's parents calmed down and apologized to me for raising their voices. They even offered to bake me some of their bread, a recipe famous to their village. Incidentally, this conversation helped Joseph's teacher appreciate how important this act of bringing her bread had been to the parents.

Naming the Problem on Page One

At this point, we took a very simple approach that I developed: we would list the problems on one side of a page, abstaining from focusing on any possible solutions. Only once this was accomplished, would we turn the paper over and think of a plan of action. This method has proven to be a highly effective tool for focusing people towards a pragmatic step-by-step approach.

So what was Joseph's problem?

Joseph had difficulties focusing during lessons and as a result, he still could not read. This was written down on the problems side of the page.

Turning the Page on the Problem, towards a Solution

Now that the problem was unanimously agreed upon, the team could form a therapeutic plan of action. We turned the page over and suddenly working towards this goal seemed much less fraught with resistance and emotional reactions.

I suggested to the parents that I evaluate Joseph to see if I had any recommendations as to how to approach his problem. According to records, his parents had been refusing testing for two years but Joseph's teacher reminded them that an evaluation did not mean that they would be mandated to medicate him. They agreed to the let me test him.

The psycho-educational evaluation showed that Joseph had the precursors for dyslexia. The main solutions, as per the recommendations, were working with a special education teacher and doing remedial homework.

After several months, and with assistance, Joseph was less evasive to working on his studies. This in turn allowed him to begin the process of developing his own strategies of learning to read.

A prescription for medication was not required.

As you can see, this stage of naming the problem is as much a clinical one, a way to troubleshoot psychological barriers, as it is a practical one, a pragmatic approach to forming a therapeutic plan, one step at a time. That is not to say that the team should be too rigid. As the collaboration continues and new evidence is brought to light, the definition of the problem may be tweaked/changed and the plan subsequently adapted.

Avoiding Medication Feuds

This example of what I call a "medication feud" is a very common one. The parents refuse to accept an academic or behavioral problem due to fear of an unacceptable or frightening solution. They may even lash out at the teacher/school system for just suggesting that there is a problem. The teacher in turn may become defensive, especially if the child is presenting with dysfunctional behaviors. This interaction can then cause the therapeutic team to start bumping heads. In the meantime, no one is naming the problem and consequentially no effective solutions can be found.

I have witnessed situations where this kind of landlocked status quo has gone on for years. The parents are upset, the teacher is upset, the child still is not given adequate solutions for their problems, and no one but no one is getting home-baked bread.

By simply taking out a piece of paper and naming problems prior to focusing on solutions, I have often been able to deescalate these feuds, steering the team towards a more effective collaboration.

Utilizing Relevant Professionals Illuminates Potential Solutions

On a side note, in these meetings, be sure to suggest involving the necessary professionals when you feel it necessary. For example, dyslexia is diagnosed by a psychologist, psychiatrist, or neurologist. Maybe there are also medical concerns? I will elaborate on this point further on. Relevant to this section is the fact that asking questions about the problem, while utilizing the relevant professionals often illuminates potential solutions.

Naming the Problem Communicates Expectations to the Child

Another reason for focusing on naming the problem is that the agreed upon problem subsequently needs to be communicated to the child. The message needs to be clear that there is an expectation that any related dysfunctional behaviors (e.g. talking to other children during a lesson) are unacceptable. Just because a dysfunctional behavior may be related to a diagnosis does not mean that it should not be named. It just means that the child in question may require a more unique solution.

Homework for the Teacher

1. Consider previous interactions with parents of a child presenting with dysfunctional behaviors. Ask yourself, were you ever part of or the witness of a medication feud?
2. Choose a student in your classroom who presents with a dysfunctional behavior and think about how you would name the problem. Just like most of the tools in this guide, this is a learned skill that requires practice. So ask yourself, what is the dysfunctional behavior? How would you describe it? Notice that the behavior can be active, like shouting in the classroom, or passive, like not preparing homework. While you do this, avoid looking for solutions and concentrate only on the problem!

3

Consider the Cause of the Behavior

Postulate a Theory about the Motivation

So far, the focus has been on the collaboration between parents and teachers, with an emphasis on enlisting parents into the collaborative triangle and naming the problem. Now we have to ask ourselves, why is this happening? This part of the intervention is best done with the active participation of the child in question.

Motivation is at the Core of Behavior

We need to consider a child's motivation for the dysfunctional behavior, since once we establish what need or want the child is fulfilling by acting in a particular way, we will be able to assist him/her in switching to a more functional way of achieving his or her goal.

A common catch phrase of mine is "say no but also say yes."

In other words, it is important to communicate when a behavior is dysfunctional (i.e. unwanted) but we should also guide a child to a more functional behavior. The behavioral approach to doing that is to first figure out the function of the dysfunctional behavior. Refer to Concept Box 3.1 for a summary of Functional Behavioral Assessments.

> **CONCEPT BOX #3.1**
>
> **Functional Behavioral Assessments**
>
> A crucial component of many behavioral methods is to hypothesize the function of a dysfunctional behavior. This method, often referred to as functional behavior assessment, is varied from clinician to clinician. Since motivation is an internal construct, any conclusion is a theory, at most.
>
> Some clinicians will interview the parents/teachers in an attempt to find out the motivation for a behavior.
>
> Could it be due to a child wanting attention?
>
> Could it be due to a need to escape from an unwanted task?
>
> Could there be a medical reason?
>
> Maybe he/she behaves in a certain way in order to get a tangible item?
>
> Many clinicians believe in the power of observation and will only hypothesize a theory regarding the motivation once they have had time to observe the behavior for themselves.
>
> Other clinicians will do more thorough assessments, where they will review all aspects related to the behavior and to the child's day-to-day schedule. They believe that performing an encompassing review of data will assist them in testing their theory.
>
> For example, take a child that behaves in a certain way only on mornings when the cafeteria is serving coleslaw. Short of the child telling us that the behavior is related to coleslaw, it would be hard to uncover this correlation without doing a exhaustive assessment.
>
> With that said, an overly thorough functional assessment can be overbearing for the child and the assessor.

Personally, I believe in following your intuition when exploring the function of a behavior. Only do a thorough assessment if you feel that you really need to.

Go with your gut.

As a teacher, you have the education and the experience relevant to this task. Your intuition has been honed by the fact that you have seen so many behaviors prior to the one you are currently seeking to modify. Trust your intuition but also be open to change your mind when new evidence comes to light.

As I have mentioned several times, not every behavior has a clear function that is effectively treatable by behavioral methods. If a child is diagnosed with a psychiatric or neurological issue then it is possible that a different therapeutic approach would be better suited.

This is not to say that The Success Diary would not be of utility, only that you would need to be sure that you are focusing on a behavior that could be changed when utilizing this method.

My rule of thumb is that if you feel comfortable about the motivation for a behavior then there is hope to change it, unless a medical/psychiatric obstacle exists that is too big for the child to overcome without professional intervention.

Truthfully, in my career I have found that it is easier to work with the more "problematic" children, the ones that may even disrupt their surroundings. This is because, even though some of their behavior is challenging, they are usually highly motivated. If guided correctly, these children can easily redirect their energies towards healthier life habits.

The children that may be more at risk are the ones that are less noticeable. The less motivated children in need, the ones that are quietly "stewing" in the background, can be much harder to reach. This difficult subject is discussed in Concept Box 3.2.

CONCEPT BOX #3.2

Recognizing an Unmotivated Child

In order to achieve success in any therapeutic intervention, the person receiving assistance needs to have a certain level of motivation. As mentioned, the child is the most important corner of the collaborative triangle. Unmotivated children are at risk since a lack of motivation markedly lowers the chances of any therapeutic intervention working.

Furthermore, if they are unmotivated to change then they may also be unmotivated to communicate distress, meaning that they are further at risk due to being easily overlooked.

One strategy to recognizing an unmotivated child is to focus on what psychologists refer to as "state" and not on "trait." In layman terms, this calls for you to refrain from comparison between children, since they naturally have different activity levels, but rather to compare a child to himself or herself.

If a child keeps to himself/herself in the classroom and seems overly passive, this does not necessarily mean that he/she is unmotivated. This could simply mean that this child is generally a more quiet person. However, if a child that is usually active is suddenly passive, then this could suggest that something is occurring with him/her. This is a child at risk of being unmotivated.

You as the teacher are the professional that is in the optimal position to monitor these children, since you would best know the activity level of all the children under your responsibility. If one of them becomes visibly more active (including dysfunctional behaviors) or visibly less active, see this as a sign for concern.

If you suspect that a child is unmotivated, or considerably less motivated than usual, an intervention may be required. This is beyond the scope of this book. If you attempt and do not succeed in motivating a child like this, consider talking to the school psychologist or school counselor.

On a side note, a good working relationship with the parents can decidedly raise the chances of identifying a child in distress, especially if you and the parents are communicating well on a steady basis.

Formulating a Theory

Investigating the motivation of dysfunctional behavior is a process of scientific discovery. Consider different options, postulate a theory, and then test it. Of course, the first step in this process should always be asking the child what he or she wants or what he or she is trying to achieve. See the following case study for a clear example of this.

About a month into the beginning of a school year, I was made aware of Sarah, a headstrong 6-year old girl, new to the first grade, who refused to enter her classroom. She would sit or stand outside the room and throw a tantrum if anyone tried to make her go in. On the rare occasions when she did go in, she would sit under her table with her back to the teacher.

This behavior started to have a negative effect on other children, some of whom had also begun sitting under tables.

Her teacher, the principal, and even her parents had tried many techniques in their attempts to get her into the classroom. This ranged from rewarding her for entering the room to having the principle talk to her. These all had varying but unsustainable results.

On observation, Sarah was a calm, strong-willed girl that clearly did not want to be in the classroom. I asked her why she refused to join the class and she said that she wanted her family to be with her.

I phoned Sarah's mother and asked her why she thought Sarah would want her family with her in the classroom. Her mother, well aware of Sarah's remarks, could not understand it. She said that Sarah had always been highly independent.

So why did she suddenly need her family at school with her?

We went through a list of common causes for this kind of sudden change, including possible minor traumas (e.g. a small car accident long forgotten by the parents) or major life events such as a loss in the family (including pets and neighbors.) Sarah's mother informed me that three months earlier her husband had lost his father, Sarah's favorite grandfather.

Behind the scenes, her father was taking it very badly but Sarah's mother assured me that Sarah never saw him cry or even exhibit a bad mood. This remark made me question what assistance Sarah had received in mourning her own loss. Why should she not see her father upset about the death of his own father?

To me, Sarah was clearly telling us that she was worried about her family, and being an intelligent and strong-willed child, she seemed to have found a way to ensure their safety, by always having them at her side. In other words, Sarah's motivation was to communicate to us that she was afraid to lose more members of her family and to find a way to protect them.

Knowledge of the Motivation for a Dysfunctional Behavior Lends Itself to Finding a Solution

Once I had formulated a theory regarding Sarah's motivation for suddenly wanting her family with her in class, I was immediately able to suggest a solution. In a six-week treatment plan, I worked with Sarah's parents on strategies to assist her in finding a more functional way of coming to terms with her loss. In the meantime, her teacher made it clear to her that Sarah could approach her to talk about her worries whenever she wanted. This way she was offered a more functional way of communicating distress.

Just a week later, Sarah agreed to enter her classroom. It was as though she had been waiting for her parents to begin this therapeutic process with her and for her teacher to understand her. In fact, Sarah's refusal to enter her classroom had culminated in another positive outcome; her father began therapy in order to process his own bereavement.

Always Start by Asking Children the Function of their Behavior

Notice that during my investigation I had consequently turned to Sarah's mother for information, but the person that had pointed me in the right direction was Sarah herself. She clearly stated to me that the issue was family. After this, everything just seemed to fall into place.

If asking the child does not work or is not an option, one could investigate whether there is anything lacking in their environment. For example, in the case of Joseph, he was going after school to an empty house. I believe that a large part of his natural motivation was to signal distress, since he was growing up in an unsupervised environment. His behavior subsequently led to his being supervised after school.

Interviewing the Parents

Yet another way of discovering the motivation for dysfunctional behavior is interviewing the parents. See the following case study for an example of this.

Michael, an 11-year-old boy, was on the verge of being expelled from his school due to his ongoing physical aggression. He was stubborn and had an irreverent attitude towards adults.

On review of the incidents, it seemed that there were two main reasons for his nearly daily fighting. He would fight with anyone who "disrespected" him in any fashion, or in order to defend his younger brother or anyone else he felt had been wronged.

At times, he would even defend the honor of people with whom he had had a physical altercation in the recent past.

His teacher informed me that despite multiple meetings, his parents refused to acknowledge that there was an issue. They were both strong-willed people, his mother a bank executive and his father a muscular fitness instructor. It was extremely difficult to get a word across with both of them in the room since they often argued with one another during the meeting. I therefore scheduled separate meetings.

During my meeting with Michael's father, it became quite apparent that he glorified his son's behavior. I discovered that two years earlier, Michael had himself been the victim of bullying by an older boy. Michael's father had not been happy about this and had told his son that he had to learn to protect himself, to "be a man" and "take care of business," and Michael had apparently complied.

It was evident that his father's views on physical aggression had a great effect on his behavior. This child was driven by a need to show that he could take care of business and the tool of choice was violence. This was my theory about the motivation.

Uncovering the Motivation for a Dysfunctional Behavior Sheds a New Light on the Behavior

Michael was now perceived not as a defiant bully, but rather a child of purpose that had gone astray. He wanted to be a protector, a strong but nice guy. He wanted to please his father.

This distinction is very important since it allows us to see him in a more positive light and lends insight into the direction that we need to take in the therapeutic plan. How could we get Michael to remain a child of purpose but in a more positive way? How could we "say no but also say yes"? Chapter 4 will elaborate on how we went about this task. Relevant to this section is how the motivation for the behavior was illuminated went interviewing the parents and how we all consequently perceived Michael differently.

The Function of a Behavior is Just One Possible Cause

There are many methods for therapeutic interventions, and although they have varying theoretical foundations, most of them include a stage of investigation. When utilizing a behavioral method, one may perform a Functional Behavioral Assessment of specific dysfunctional behaviors. When practicing psychodynamic therapy, a therapist will usually analyze the underlying causes of patterns of behavior. Psychologists, psychiatrists, and various medical doctors implement a stage of diagnosis.

Before moving forward, the team will want to ensure that they have considered all possible causes for a behavior. These factors are no less important than postulating a theory for the motivation for a behavior.

What is the difference between a cause and the function you ask?

As mentioned, the function of the behavior is what the child is trying to achieve. In other words, what is their goal? This is one type of cause for a behavior but there are a plethora of hypothetical causes for behavior that are not directly related to the function of the behavior. These are determinants that may not be under the control of the child (for example, medical).

Let us look at the example of Donna, a 6-year-old girl, who would yell at any student, whenever they walked passed her desk. Sometimes, she would even yell at the teacher. When asked why she was behaving this way, she said that it was because she was trying to concentrate on her work. Her parents subsequently took her for a psychological evaluation and she was diagnosed with attention deficit disorder.

In this case, the function of the behavior was related to her attempts at focusing on a lesson but the main cause of the behavior was the difficulty in conentration due to her diagnosis. This is actually a common phenomenon for children with attention deficit disorder. If they are disturbed when trying to concentrate in class, it is challenging for them to return their focus to their studies.

Now let us look at a another example, where the function of the behavior is similar but the cause is different. Emma, a 7-year-old girl, was having difficulty paying attention in class, presenting with the behavior of constantly asking questions unrelated to the subject matter being taught. She was especially disruptive to the students surrounding her desk, since she would ask them questions too; therefore, she had been seated on the far right side of the class.

Of course, the question of attention deficit disorder had previously been brought up; however, this had been ruled out by a psychologist.

I asked Emma why she was asking so many questions and she said that she wanted to understand the lesson. I postulated a theory that the function of the behavior was to concentrate on the lesson.

A common practice of mine, when working with a family, is to request that parents check their children's hearing and vision and I did so in this case too. Consequently, it was discovered that Emma had a medical condition causing intermittent hearing loss in her left ear. As stated she was seated on the far right side of the classroom (i.e. with the teacher to the left of her). This suggested that the cause of her behavior was due to her inability to hear the teacher.

Both of these case studies portray a situation where the function of similar behaviors was a child wanting to concentrate but subsequently it was found that the underlying causes of the behaviors were divergent. Donna was diagnosed with attention deficit disorder, whereas Emma had a medical condition that was causing hearing problems.

Uncovering the Cause for the Behavior May Suggest Non-behavioral Solutions

In my experience, knowledge of a possible cause for behavior often lends itself to a non-behavioral solution. For example, a small operation fixed Donna's hearing problem and as a result, her academic achievements rose steadily. This is a medical solution.

Emma's parents did not feel comfortable medicating her; however, her teacher moved her to an area in the class where children walking by would not easily disturb her. This was an environmental solution.

For further example, a child having mini seizures is going to benefit more from seeing a neurologist. A child suffering from depression would require seeing a mental health professional.

This, however, is not to say that a behavioral intervention such as The Success Diary would not be helpful as a supplementary aide. For example, a child diagnosed with dyslexia may need an individualized education plan. A Success Diary could supplement this treatment by focusing on keeping the child motivated to study, especially since he or she will probably need to study more hours than other children. Take into account that for this to work, one would need to identify a dysfunctional behavior regarding studying habits and not postulate a theory regarding a child's motivation for not being able to read, as this is not a behavior.

Homework for the Teacher

1. In the previous chapter you practiced naming a problem for a child you know that is presenting with dysfunctional behavior. Now try and think of possible causes for the behavior, including the function of the behavior. Remember, the function is what the child is trying to achieve; whereas, the possible causes are more far reaching, including medical, environmental, emotional, psycho-educational, and so on.

4

Finding Alternatives to Dysfunctional Behavior

Define a Required Skill Set

So now, you have named the problem and you have a theory as to why a child is motivated to behave in a particular way. The latter included the crucial step of asking the children why they are behaving the way they do. Once the motivation is clear, we can often find a fairly simple solution (e.g. minor ear surgery). In other situations, we will need to devise a more systematic therapeutic plan.

There are many different ways to approach the problem once it has been named and a therapeutic plan of action is required. One of the options would be the implementation of a Success Diary. The role of The Success Diary is to monitor and reinforce the practice of relevant skill sets. Defining this set of skills to work on is the final prerequisite prior to implementation.

Reinforcing Skills and not Behaviors

You may notice that at this stage I describe skills and not behaviors. This is because I find that doing so allows the team to turn their focus towards growth, as the quality of the discourse becomes more personalized. Remember that this is a crucial element of The Success Diary approach.

Behaviors are not about who we are but rather about our actions, whereas skill sets are part of us. "Good" behavior is very often about satisfying someone else, and not necessarily about our own capabilities. Proficiency at a skill contributes to a person's sense of capability.

Motivating Parents to Believe in Change

Parents do not always believe that their child is capable of or even should change their dysfunctional behavior. Although the task of getting parents to believe in change is not necessarily in the scope of a teacher's job, doing so can facilitate a behavioral intervention.

The follow up to the case study of Michael portrays one way of doing this. During my meeting with Michael's father he had shared that he was proud of his son's ability to protect himself and others. He believed that being strong is an important part of development. This sentiment was likely reinforcing Michael's urge to fight.

In order to achieve a positive change, it was necessary to enlist his father into creating a different developmental environment. In other words, his father needed to believe that Michael can and should change.

To this purpose, I made use of re-framing (refer to Concept Box 4.1 for further elaboration on this technique). In a follow up meeting with the father, I agreed with him that his son needed to protect himself. If Michael had gone from being bullied to being able to protect himself then of course, his father should be proud of him.

Not only that, once he had made it clear to the school at large that he would not be bullied, he had begun to protect other children.

I wondered, however, whether Michael had not taken it too far. His father agreed that Michael could tone it down a bit, but he confided in me that he did not know how to get his son to do so. I suggested that implementing a Success Diary as a behavioral intervention could prove effective.

CONCEPT BOX #4.1

Re-framing and Saying "No" with a Smile

Working as a school psychologist, I learnt to be aware of my impact on other people's lives. I became cognizant of the fact that I was a service provider. This was a difficult position to be in, since a large part of my job was to reflect to people patterns in their behavior, which includes assisting them in seeing their own negative emotions and their own dysfunctional behavior.

Two of my mentors equipped me with tools to resolve this conundrum. The first taught me ways to re-frame and the other taught me how to say no.

Re-framing is a highly complex therapeutic tool that I will only touch upon. Think of this method as a way of agreeing with people instead of confronting them on an error they are making. In other words, if a parent provides justification for a dysfunctional behavior then think how you can make that justification into a positive plan of action. A trick to doing this is to find a way to state your case starting with a "yes," no matter the circumstances.

If a father believes that his son should be physically aggressive at school in order to defend himself, tell him "yes, he should be safe but is there another way?"

If the mother of a daughter that suffers from an eating disorder states that she simply wants to look good, tell her "yes, looking good is important, but is there a way to do so while also developing healthier eating habits?"

If parents believe that other children are rejecting their child because of their racial background, tell them "yes, it is possible that there is racially driven bias against your child. Maybe, with the assistance of the teacher, there is a way to make this into a learning opportunity for everyone in the classroom?"

If a child is non-compliant with his/her own therapeutic plan, tell him/her "yes, it is your choice if you want to take part. Do you think that you are making a good decision?"

All of these real life examples were resolved because I used re-framing. I did not confront the person involved on what he or she believed/feared but rather found a way to agree with them.

After that we were able to become a team and to be solution focused.

As you will see when attempting this technique yourself, this is a simple goal but extremely complex in execution.

Re-framing requires patience, empathy, and creativity. It is a learned skill that requires constant practice. With that said, it is worth the effort. Straight-on confrontation very often is counterproductive and leads to resistance, but finding a positive common ground is the first step in collaborating towards a workable solution.

Once re-framing has been used with a parent or child, and a plan of action is being put in place, we can then start discussing apparent obstacles to the plan. Now the focus is on the positive while taking into account the negative.

This is in comparison to just mentioning the dysfunctional behavior, which could be seen as simply focusing on the negative. The latter approach may be perceived as a personal attack, especially with people that are feeling insecure regarding the issue at hand.

Sometimes, using re-framing is just not an option and we have to find a way to say "no." For example, if parents are requesting something unreasonable like two extra teachers in the classroom or the removal of another child from the class.

In these cases, I refer to another mentor of mine who had an admirable talent of saying "no" to anyone in such a way that they would accept it. His secret was to say it with a contagious smile.

This simple technique requires very specific interpersonal skills. You need to be able to build a rapport with someone very quickly, making him or her feel immediately at ease. Other than that, you need to be confident in

> your response and not to be over apologetic. I think that you need to convey that you are saying "no" but that you are open to other solutions.
>
> To sum up, when encountering the need to point out to someone an error that they are making, try to re-frame, starting with a "yes." Do not be confrontational but rather find a way to agree with them. If this fails then tell them "no" but with a smile.

As mentioned in the previous chapter, Michael's dysfunctional behavior of physical aggression, which we had named as fighting too much, seemed to be motivated by a need to protect himself and others. The next stage of the intervention was to meet with Michael and define a skill set to work on.

Informing the Child what the Problem is and Suggesting a Change

The goal of The Success Diary is to reinforce a specific skill set as an alternative to presenting with a dysfunctional behavior. The skill set is defined with the collaboration of the child and in order to do so, the child first needs to know what the problem is. This may have been discussed when inquiring into the motivation of the behavior but now a clear line is being drawn in the sand.

Children will be hesitant to take part in a discussion of their dysfunctional behavior and therefore a positive approach is preferred. For example, prior to this specific meeting, as a way to enlist Michael into the collaborative triangle, his father had a conversation with him, telling him that he was proud of him for learning how to defend himself.

During the meeting, we informed Michael that we all wanted him to fight less.

Initially, he was resistant to us, stating that it was not his fault. There were many bullies in the school and he was just protecting himself and other students.

His teacher told him that he was right to defend himself and that he was a great guy for protecting other students. She wondered, however, maybe he did not always need to go straight to physical aggression as this did hurt other children? Maybe there were other ways to assist his classmates?

Notice how she changed the word "protect" to "assist."

Michael reacted with a lot of optimism to his teacher's words. Until then he had always been told that fighting is bad. No one wanted to see things from his perspective. As far as he was concerned, he was being a nice guy. He had a self-defined skill (i.e. protecting himself by fighting) and he wanted to use it for the benefit of others.

I reiterated the teacher's words that he could assist his friends, just maybe in alternative ways by utilizing a different skill set. He agreed to use a Success Diary, which I described as a personal tool to help him focus on achieving this goal.

Defining a Skill Set

We defined the following skill set to practice: assist another student peacefully; be polite to a teacher; help my younger brother get to class on time. These were all things that he could do in order to achieve his goal of being a nice guy and be of benefit to others, while not having to resort to violence.

Defining skills allows us to put a positive spin on the dysfunctional behavior. Michael's behavior of fighting with other children was at least in part an expression of his need to be a nice guy, by trying to protect other children.

We did not treat this sentiment as an excuse/justification for his behavior but rather as the driving force. We then found another way for him to be a nice guy, by suggesting he develop new skills to replace or at least augment his old skill of defending others. In this case, we re-framed his motivation as assisting others.

Notice that we did not have to delve too deep in to reasons why the behavior of fighting is negative. The reason for the meeting was a sufficient rebuke to his behavior of fighting. The focal point of the meeting was developing the skill set consistent with the function of the behavior.

As you can see, defining skill sets can be quite complex. It requires an ability to re-frame negative ways of achieving a goal in a positive way. I suggest taking your time and practicing thinking of skill sets until you feel comfortable enough to start applying this technique in a real life scenario. The following guidelines may assist you in this task:

1. Consider the child's clinical background (e.g. age; strengths; weaknesses; functioning level; social abilities). The skill set should be graspable for a child but also not so simplistic as to be insulting. Sometimes this is just a question of wording. For example, being nice is different from being a positive force in the classroom, which is different from being an ethical member of society.
2. The skill set should be somewhat measurable. Will you be able to intuitively mark whether a child has succeeded in using the skill or not? For example, thinking positive thoughts cannot easily be measured but making positive remarks can be.
3. I usually select three skills to put in a skill set, although this depends on the child and the case. Focusing on too many skills at a time can be discouraging. If there are many things the child needs to work on then it is better to focus on one skill set at a time, maybe implementing another Success Diary a few months later. For example, for a child that is presenting with physical aggression and non-compliance with homework, you could first focus on one and then the other.
4. Define a skill set that is difficult to attain but still achievable. For example, for a 5-year-old child that is non-compliant with homework, you would not define a skill of autonomously doing homework alone every day. On the other hand, for a 13-year-old child with the same behavior, you would not define a skill of doing homework with mommy before bedtime.

5. If a child has low self-esteem, define one of the skills as something that he or she is already good at. This will assist in motivation. For example, Michael was good at history so another skill could have been helping someone else with history homework.
6. A defined skill set should include skills that you believe that a child needs in order not to present with the dysfunctional behavior in question. This is the core idea behind the method of defining a skill set. For example, a child that leaves the classroom without asking permission may need to work on a skill related to self-control or communication, depending on the motivation for the behavior. Is the child doing this because he/she does not want to be told what to do or is this just a case of a forgetful child needing the bathroom?
7. The skill set should be collaboratively defined. Optimally, the parents and you guide a child in defining their own skill set, using some of their own words in the final wording. The ratio of guidance to children's own input really varies from case to case. Just remember that the goal is for them to adopt the skill set as their own, but to also feel that they were assisted in defining this skill set that they need to improve in. Michael's case study is a great example of fruitful collaboration on this task.
8. Learn about the child's likes and be creative. I once worked with a child that would run out of class to play with insects, stating that books could not teach him anything. I defined the skill as learning about insects from a book and provided him with a fun book about insects.

When it comes to defining a skill set, there is no right answer. Really, it just has to make sense. Will learning this skill set likely teach the child a better way of achieving their goal?

Before moving forward to create a Success Diary, make sure that you are comfortable with the chosen skill set. If you are having too many issues or the team cannot come to agreement then do not move on to the next stage. This would be the time to seek assistance from another professional, like a psychologist or counselor.

Another Example of the Steps to Defining a Skill Set

Here is an example that takes us through the steps of naming the problem, postulating a theory for the motivation of the behavior, and defining a skill set. Angela, a 14-year-old girl, was stealing candy from her classmates. She had been caught on numerous occasions, and when I asked her why she was stealing, she said it was because her mother refused to have sugar in the house.

Her teacher and I met with the mother and began to easily collaborate. She was an easygoing woman, full of energy. She stated that she had taken Angela for some testing and that there was no medical reason for her having the urge to steal candy.

I inquired into the issue of candy and the family's nutritional habits in general. Her mother informed me that she had implemented a sugar-free household about six months earlier.

We named the problem as Angela acquiring and eating food that contained sugar. The teacher and I would have preferred to define the problem as stealing candy but Angela's mother did not like the negative connotation and preferred to focus on the sugar consumption aspect of the behavior. We compromised.

In a private conversation, the teacher and I noted that a possible cause of the behavior was the sudden change in nutritional habits, an environmental cause. Angela's teacher did not directly bring this up with the mother but rather used re-framing. She agreed with Angela's mother that healthy nutrition was very important to Angela's lifestyle. She then wondered if there was a way of implementing this new life habit in a manner that motivated Angela to take part.

We sat together with Angela and had a discussion on the benefits of having a healthy lifestyle. Conceptually, she understood the importance of it, but said that she liked candy and wanted to carry on eating it. She did not think that her mother should tell her what to eat.

My theory was that the behavior was motivated by a need for tangibles (i.e. candy). Angela wanted control over her nutritional habits. I agreed with her that having a choice in her own eating habits is important, but suggested that maybe she was making bad decisions by stealing. I then told her that I wanted her to experience how enjoyable healthy eating habits can be. She agreed to try a Success Diary in pursuit of this goal.

I defined the following new skill set: eating healthy snacks from a selection of snacks; sharing healthy snacks with classmates; learning about nutrition. She would work on these skills in order to modify her behavior.

Notice how Angela's skills were opposites of the dysfunctional behaviors: eating candy and stealing from classmates. Yet, notice also that practicing these skills does allow a level of control. She could choose her snacks from a selection of snacks, she got to choose whom she shares with, and learning about nutrition would enrich her own decision making.

An Example of Defining a Skill Set without Collaboration of the Parents

Here is another simple example of defining a skill set but this time without the assistance of the parents. Elaine, a 15-year-old girl, had been steadily doing less and less homework throughout the year and now was failing in most of her classes.

Following a few attempts at meeting them, her parents made it clear that they were not interested in collaborating with Elaine's teacher and me. We decided to do the best we could without their assistance.

Her teacher sat down with her and asked why she was not doing her homework. Elaine said that she was too busy working as a waitress after school.

Her teacher queried her as to why she felt the need to work so much. Initially, she said that she had to earn money for herself, since her parents did not give her an allowance. After further discussion, she confided that she did not believe she would finish high school due to her low grades. She was working as a waitress, since she knew that those were the kind of jobs she would be doing for the rest of her life. It is important to note that her mother worked as a waitress as well.

The teacher took Elaine for weekly pep talks, and after about a month, Elaine agreed to try a Success Diary.

The hypothesis was that her behavior of not making an effort in her studies was motivated by a need to find her place in the world. Confident that she was not meant to have an occupation that required even minimal academic skills, as far as she was concerned, she had already begun to pursue her chosen career.

The skill set that was consequently defined was the following: doing homework; taking an interest in something academic; learning about my options in life.

Notice how these are skills that are focused on allowing for development as opposed to just practicing a new behavior. I believe that only defining the behavior of doing homework would have made a positive outcome less probable since it so impersonal. Children need to be able to relate to the goals that we set them.

Skill Sets are about Personal Growth

Anyone acquainted with methods of Applied Behavior Analysis will recognize the similarities between these methods and The Success Diary. A dysfunctional behavior is replaced in compliance with the function of the behavior. One of the main differences, as stated, is the emphasis on the reinforcement of a skill set and not on a specific concrete behavior, as is generally common practice for applied behavior analysts.

In pure behavioral methods, the need for the child's awareness of the behavior being reinforced is not of big concern. The Success Diary approach, on the other hand, puts dialogue with the child in the forefront, including encouraging participation in the various steps of planning the intervention. In this way, this method resembles cognitive behavioral approaches, which often integrate the learning of skills into therapeutic interventions (usually while working with a therapist).

This is not to say that at times it is unbeneficial to focus on behaviors. If a child is presenting with dysfunctional behavior we need to be able to recognize it. Remember, this kind of behavior can very often be seen as a form of communication. Furthermore, behavior provides a concrete way of confronting a child (e.g. it is very easy to grasp that stealing is unacceptable).

On the other hand, when looking for a solution to the problem, focusing on skill sets provides, among other benefits, a way of enlisting a child into his or her own therapeutic plan. As mentioned, we need to motivate the child to actively pursue this goal of positive change.

In other words, say no but also say yes, by saying no to dysfunctional behaviors and yes to functional skill sets.

Another advantage of focusing on skills is that it raises our ability to overcome resistance in the form of oppositional behavior. Many children will show defiance when asked to stop a behavior.

Sometimes this is because they feel that we do not understand why they are behaving the way they are and sometimes this is simply a knee-jerk reaction. In the latter case, a behavior may have become a button issue representing much more than just a behavior.

Doing homework becomes so much more than just the act of opening a book.

Not eating candy represents so much more than just a nutritional choice.

Washing dishes becomes so much more than just a hygienic chore.

By focusing more on skills that need to be learned, rather than on changing dysfunctional behavior, we change the script.

The dialogue becomes about personal growth and not about being good or bad. This in turn allows us to lean more on the tools of psychological treatment theories (both cognitive behavioral and psychodynamic).

By personalizing the intervention and allowing a child to be an active part of all stages of the therapeutic plan we can do what any therapist does, listen to the children's voice, allow them space for a personal process of growth, and guide them when needed. See Concept Box 4.2 for a discussion on self-sustaining transformations, the goal of most therapy.

CONCEPT BOX #4.2

The Parameters of a Self-sustaining Transformation

When performing a therapeutic intervention, you want to ensure that the goal is a self-sustaining transformation. This means that you are providing a child with a temporary support system but that the intended outcome is the ability to maintain the results without this support system.

For example, when providing therapy for a child that has disproportionate emotional reactions to every day occurrences, the therapist may work with the child on gaining a stronger level of emotional regulation.

Initially, they would review examples of upsetting incidents and extreme emotional reactions; however, with time the expectation would be that the child learns to fittingly adapt his/her emotional responses to occurrences in his/her life without having to review it with the therapist.

In order to achieve a self-sustaining transformation for the current type of educational intervention, try to confine yourself to the following parameters:

1. Put a deadline on the intervention. I like to have a sixteen-week deadline for a Success Diary, although this can obviously vary from child to child. If you reach the end of the intervention period and there was no progress, you still need to end it at the intended time.
2. Keep the intervention within the chosen context. The Success Diary is not intended to touch on every

component of a child's life. The intention is to monitor and reinforce a specific skill set. If a child is currently using a Success Diary to address the behavior of fighting, then another behavior (e.g. not doing homework) is not strictly relevant. In fact, if child starts referring to an unrelated behavior in regards to their Success Diary, you should correct him or her.

3. Do not make an overbearing intervention. Many behavior charts have what I consider an oppressive amount of monitoring sessions. Many going as far as to have a child monitored throughout the entire day. The child may feel that this intervention is unpleasant and have less motivation. The teacher too may be overwhelmed by the intervention, if it requires too many hours of monitoring. This is counterproductive and not conducive to a self-sustaining transformation. We want to provide children with a few sessions where they actively practice on gaining their skill sets, but we also want to give them ample opportunity to experience real life changes at times when they are not being monitored. Think about this: if a child that needs to learn to assist others is suddenly utilizing that skill during times that he/she is not being monitored, we have strong evidence that the intervention is working.

4. Finally, the intervention should be personal. The child needs to know that their Success Diary is not about behaving in a way that pleases the environment. It is about personal development. This sentiment should be reiterated throughout the intervention.

Keep in mind that the parameters that I have mentioned here are specific to The Success Diary. Other types of interventions would require a different setting.

Furthermore, it is important to be flexible when working with children. They may openly say that they want different parameters. This is fine, as long as the parameters make sense and are decided on when preparing

> The Success Diary and not after the intervention has already begun.
>
> Once you have started the monitoring stage presented in Chapter 7, you as the teacher want to be the driving force that ensures all parties stay on task. This ensures a stable intervention, where expectations are consistent. Otherwise a child may try to manipulate the intervention later on.

Homework for the Teacher

1. Consider parents that have made statements to you that suggest that they do not believe that their child can change. How would you re-frame the statement to motivate them to believe in change?
2. Identify three children in your classroom that you believe you know the motivation for a dysfunctional behavior that they are each presenting with. Try and define a separate skill set for each one.

5

Time to Address the Dysfunctional Behavior

Make a Success Diary

A collaborative triangle has been formed, the problem has been named, a motivation for the behavior has been postulated, and a skill set, which the child has to practice on, has been defined. Now you can go ahead and make a Success Diary. This is done in a step-by-step fashion that is quite simple.

Step One: Select a Notebook with the Child

The Success Diary is owned by the child and ideally he/she should pick his/her own physical book. It is important that the notebook has at least twenty blank double-sided pages (i.e. forty pages) and be no smaller than approximately A5 in page size.

Going to the store might be overwhelming for some children, so it may be more advisable to purchase a few possible diaries and offer these to the child in private. The important thing is that he/she feels that a personal choice has been made.

The problem with many behavior modification charts is that they do not belong to the child. They are usually hung on the wall/fridge or held by the teacher/parent. This can give a child the sense that the chart is a tool for others to monitor his/her behavior and not a tool to be utilized for a personal process of growth.

Giving the child the freedom to choose the book is a milestone in relaying an understanding that it belongs to him/her.

It is important to consistently convey this to a child. You do this with words and with actions. You should refer to it as "your Success Diary." When you want to review the book, you ask for it. You do not force it.

In fact, if in a fit of rage a child decides to rip the book up, you allow him/her to do so. It is his/her book. You later review together why he/she got so frustrated and offer to buy another book in order to start from scratch (if you still believe the child capable).

Step Two: Develop the Monitoring Schedule without the Child

Decide on monitoring sessions according to a schedule that is consistent (e.g. daily; same amount of sessions per week), if possible, slightly varied (i.e. not at the same time every day), and not overbearing (no more than two sessions a day). This is done without input from the child.

Usually the sessions occur twice a day, one full lesson at a time, Monday to Friday. However, the sessions can be during breaks or during transitions (coming to or leaving school), depending on the skill defined and the dysfunctional behavior being addressed. For example, a child that is hiding in the bushes when the end of break bell rings would be monitored during these time periods.

The benefit of making the monitoring schedule slightly irregular from day to day is based on theories of conditioning and learning. Methods and practices of Applied Behavior Analysis are largely based on these theories. Varying the times of the monitoring sessions raises the probability of a skill being learned and then generalized out of the monitoring sessions (i.e. utilized at other times).

There are only two monitoring sessions a day, in order to ensure The Success Diary is effective but moderate. The intervention is only a part of the child's life and not representative of his/her entire day. Remember, the purpose is to practice a skill set, which in turn will naturally modify behavior, and not to forcefully modify specific behaviors.

Make a table for the monitoring schedule where the rows represent skills and the columns show the days and times of all of the sessions of one week.

Make sixteen copies of the table (i.e. corresponding to sixteen weeks) in the book, pages four to thirty-four, only on even pages. On the top of each of these pages, write down the start date of the intervention, week in the intervention (e.g. 1/16), and end date of the intervention.

Putting all of the pages into The Success Diary prior to using it is important since we, firstly, want to communicate a predefined period of growth and, secondly, that we are expecting that an effort be made.

Step Three: Present The Success Diary to the Child

Meet in private with the child and show him/her the changes you have made to The Success Diary. Initially the purpose is to reiterate the reason for the implementation of this method: the child needs to work on practicing a new skill set.

Start by having a conversation with the child, discussing the book as a tool for personal growth.

Turn to the first table and discuss each skill with the child. At this point that conversation has already occurred but this recap is important since it connects the context of those discussions with the material book itself.

Following that, present all of the tables that you put into the book. Children, especially younger ones, can be very concrete in their thinking. I find that it is best to explain the sheet in a step-by-step sequence: specifically, how long a monitoring session is, when the monitoring will occur, and how long the entire intervention will go on for.

Depending on many factors, including age, children will have varying levels of understanding of this tool. There is no need for them to fully comprehend these concepts. You may need to refresh these details later on when implementing the intervention so do not worry if it seems as if the child does not grasp all aspects of the process. The important thing is that the child understands that it belongs to him/her and that specific skills are being monitored.

For example, for a 6-year-old girl the message could be that with her Success Diary she can see that she is able to sit quietly through a whole lesson (at a time). On the other hand, for a 16-year-old boy the message could be an explanation of your sincere belief that he is capable of attending a disliked lesson and that his Success Diary is a way to portray this point.

Step Four: Encourage the Child to Personalize his/her Success Diary

Now that the purpose of The Success Diary has been established, we want to make it personal, thus encouraging ownership of the intervention. Have the child write his/her name on the cover, providing assistance if need be. Some children like to add personal markings or notations. Some write "My Success Diary," others graffiti their name on the cover, and others use a stencil. It is personal property so all of this is perfectly acceptable.

If a child wants to put something negative on the cover try to encourage making it more positive but do not force the issue. For example, Angela wanted to write "Angela's Fat Book" on the cover, since she said that it made her laugh. Her teacher agreed that humor is a great coping skill but that Angela had previously confided that she did not like it when other children made jokes about her weight. The teacher suggested that she might not continue to see the statement as funny on days when she was struggling towards her goals. Together they thought of a funny sentence that was not negative. Angela ended up writing "Angela's Sugar Book" on the front and covered the rest of it with stickers of candy.

After writing a name on the cover, ask the child to start decorating The Success Diary. He/she can embellish it anywhere except on the tables. Some children like to put stickers on the odd pages, others like to draw, and a few write personal notes.

I have had a couple cases where the child suddenly wanted to wrap a new cover on the book. This is not just fine. It is wonderful! The more creative they get, the better.

I truly believe that creativity has a healing effect. Creativity is growth and this is what we are asking the child to do.

For children that require a bit more structure/encouragement, it is okay to assist them with personalizing their Success Diary. You can also ask their parents to sit with them and make it into an activity. Or you can separate the task of decorating the book into sessions. Some teachers would ask a child to decorate one page a week. For example, if they were using the monitoring sheet on page 8 that week, then the child would be asked to decorate the opposite page (i.e. page 7).

Truthfully, just like any intervention, The Success Diary method is based on objective theoretical concepts. Ownership, a belief in change, and personal understanding only truly occur after subjective experience.

This step of personalizing the diary is of extreme importance since a child that sees his/her Success Diary as personal will more likely benefit from this intervention. This is easier said than done. Encouraging a sense of ownership is not a simple process, especially if you are trying to enlist a child into owning an item that he/she may not initially want or comprehend.

Troubleshooting is Part of the Job

As you can see, preparing a Success Diary at this point is quite straightforward; however, you will find that various unforeseen issues can arise. I could provide you with an extensive list of obstacles that you may encounter and possible solutions for troubleshooting but I do not think that this would be beneficial. Everyone defines obstacles differently and we all approach problems from our own perspectives. It would be better for you to trust your capability as a teacher and follow your own intuition.

As stated in the introduction, this guide delineates an approach to behaviors that you as the teacher are already forced to deal with. Through your training and experience you are already equipped with a valid, professional viewpoint.

This book is just a guide to assist you in honing your personal skills. You are capable. If these statements are of concern to you, please refer to Concept Box 5.1.

CONCEPT BOX #5.1

The Mindfulness Bottle

Teaching is a stressful job. Therefore, I thought it prudent to include a section about managing anxiety. To do so, I would like to present an analogy that I developed, The Mindfulness Bottle.

As a bottle retains water, so your body retains stress. Throughout the day, stress (the water) fills your body (the bottle). Examples of causes of stress include cars honking, project deadlines, social expectations, personal desires not met, and so on.

If stress levels are very high then the slightest nudge can cause "overflow."

For children this would be a temper tantrum. For adults it's more complex: agitation, panic attacks, different forms of escape from reality (e.g. excessive drinking; watching too much TV; cracking inappropriate jokes) and so on.

Trying to relax at this point can easily be counterproductive. The body goes into fight-or-flight mode and works on automatic. Trying to force yourself to relax can actually cause more anxiety. So what should you do?

Easy. Take a sip!

Take a sip every day before you get there.

"Take a sip" meaning do something that relaxes you.

By lowering your stress levels on a daily basis you lower the chances of overflow.

What you need to do is train yourself not to get to this point of overflow.

Do you swim, meditate, listen to music, make art, practice Tai chi, run your dog at the park, arrange flowers, or anything else that is focused on you and your bodily need to relax? It is important that you make space for personal time to let your mind and body lower stress levels.

When you do take this time and perform one of these activities, make sure to take note of your level of stress. It is important to be able recognize when you are relaxed.

Then, during the day, take a moment from time to time again to notice your stress level (e.g. is your heart beating a bit faster or your chest muscles tightening when one of the children starts pouring milk on the new carpet?)

Being aware of your body (including stress levels) and your thoughts is an integral part of mindfulness. By raising this self-awareness you are more likely to recognize when your stress levels are approaching overflow.

I personally walk around with a water bottle as a constant reminder to monitor my own stress levels. And when I exercise, I tell myself that by doing this for myself, I am also doing the world a favor. Nobody likes an anxious psychologist.

Homework for the Teacher

1. Make a mock-up table for one of the three children that you practiced defining skill sets for (in the previous chapter).
2. Consider how you would hypothetically enlist that child into personalizing their Success Diary. What suggestions would you make?

6

Improving Behavior
Encourage a Sense of Capability

Before moving on, I want to elaborate on the key concept behind The Success Diary. As mentioned, this tool utilizes behavioral techniques to reinforce the learning of a defined skill set in order to diminish the occurrence of specific dysfunctional behaviors. As it is optimally developed in collaboration with the parents, the communication of expectations is being kept consistent. Both of these elements, an appropriately defined skill set as well as clear communication, are crucial to the intervention but there is one more aspect that is indispensable to the effectiveness of the tool. With The Success Diary, you can assist a child in gaining a sense of capability.

It Generally Takes More than Clear Expectations to Modify Dysfunctional Behavior

Once you, as a team, have defined a skill set, the child should be aware of what is expected of him/her, especially since both you, the teacher and his/her parents are, at this point, clearly communicating these expectations. If this is the case, then theoretically speaking should not the child subsequently change his/her ways immediately? Why do we even need a Success Diary at this point at all?

Well, unfortunately, even when expectations are properly and consistently communicated, most children will not change their behavior. This transformation is a process with two main obstacles, the first being the inherent effort in learning a new skill.

We all know how hard it is to train ourselves into a new habit (e.g. eating a healthy breakfast), while breaking an old one (e.g. drinking coffee and grabbing three donuts on the way to work).

The behavioral aspects of the intervention address this first obstacle. As you will see in Chapter 7, an integral part of the intervention is consistently providing positive reinforcement when the child practices a skill. This encouragement raises motivation levels, making change more reachable.

The second obstacle is that many children have a low sense of capability.

Michael may have felt that he does not know how to resolve conflict without fighting.

Elaine clearly stated that as far as she was concerned, she was not academically capable.

Angela may have believed that she was not capable of staying away from candy.

Measuring Personal Capability in a Skill Set is in Itself a Learned Skill

In general, people often measure their own capabilities in an erroneous fashion. For children this is even more evident since they have had less experience in measuring what they are capable of doing.

Let us look at the example of learning to write in order to illustrate this point. We know that, barring any serious roadblocks, almost all children will learn to write in school. This is obvious to us since we have experienced this ourselves. But is it obvious to the children?

Try and remember yourself as you went through your many years of education.

Kindergartners will generally know how to write their names, but when they encounter a child in the second grade, they may not believe themselves capable of learning how to write a full paragraph.

Second graders may be capable of doing this but when encountering a fifth grader, they may not believe themselves capable of learning how to write pages of difficult words.

Fifth graders may be capable of doing this, but when encountering someone in college they may think it impossible that they would ever be able to generate what seems to them like books and books of complex text.

Now extend this example of learning to every aspect of human learning, including social, emotional, academic, physical, artistic, and so on.

Until we reach our highest potential, we do not really know what we are capable of doing. Even then, we may be mistaken, since it is possible that what we perceive as our highest potential is just an illusion.

A sense of capability is a complex calculation in the brain (refer to Concept Box 6.1 for an elaboration on this subject). Just like any complex calculation, we often make errors. In my experience, most people are more capable than what they perceive and then sometimes, people perceive themselves as skilled at a level they, unfortunately, cannot or have yet to achieve.

CONCEPT BOX #6.1

Forming Positive Memories of a Skill Set

A skill set, in the context of this guide, is a list of cognitive "components" required in order to perform a specific task (e.g. reading requires recognizing letters, recognizing words, computing grammar, deliberating on context, and so on). I believe that self-perception of one's own capability in performing a task is a component of the skill set required to perform said task, something that is learned through experience. The collaborative triangle, through the use of The Success Diary, can positively affect the quality of this learning experience for children.

To elaborate on this, a short primer on memory is required. From the point of view of cognitive psychology, memory is more than recorded episodes of things that have occurred to us. It is a complex neural representation (network), an archive of information that is at the basis of cognitive functioning.

Memory is what we do, what we see, what we think, what we feel, and so much more.

It is more than just remembering things that have happened; it is the way we form actions and perceptions. We generally take specific actions according to a memorized plan of action (e.g. the action of washing a cup follows somewhat the same sequence of movements each time we do it).

Regarding perception, we recognize what we see based on previous exposure (e.g. we recognize a cat because we have seen cats before; we recognize our spouse's voice because of all the times we have heard them before).

Finally, memory is also the framework for complex thought, often referred to as executive functioning.

In ways, there is a similarity between memory in the brain and memory in computers.

Data, which is everything we have experienced and are currently experiencing, is archived, processed, and acted upon. As you can see, this memory can theoretically be divided into different categories such as procedures (action plans), perception (e.g. what objects look/smell/feel like), personal episodes (e.g. the first time I met my wife).

When we think about a skill, this can activate memory of aspects related to this skill. For example, with the memory of driving, other than the procedures required (e.g. steering; navigating in a large environment), we will be a bit more conscious of everything associated to driving. This can include scanning for dangers, the smell and look of our car, the feeling of stress due to traffic jams, the sense of freedom driving allows, our perception of our own driving capability, and so on.

What is important to remember about memories is that they are not necessarily crystallized, or set in stone. Memory can be fluid, something that develops over time, especially for children that are still forming so many memories for the first time (i.e. constantly learning new skills and perceptions).

Relevant to this guide is the emotional/self-perceptual context associated to the memory of a skill while it is being formed. How we perform a skill is very much affected by concomitant factors, including how capable we feel.

This is where The Success Diary comes in. It brings into focus a child's perception of his/her capability when performing a skill that is being developed. In other words, the skill needs to be associated with a gradual growth in his/her sense of capability. This in turn will motivate a child to further learn the skill, aiming for maximum personal potential.

Another way to look at it is that memory networks become more multifaceted as we grow. Initially, memories are simplistic and as they are formed (consolidated) they become more complex.

For example, the first few times we see a cat we will start to recognize what a cat is. With time, we will start to recognize different types of cats (e.g. Siamese) and even specific cats (e.g. the neighbors' cat). If we move on to learn biology we may come to recognize different feline species and subspecies.

The described is a natural process of development where a network of memories becomes more complex and adaptable with time.

One can apply the same logic for the component of memory related to a sense of capability in a specific skill set. As children we initially measure capability in a skill simply as binary. We perceive ourselves as either capable or not capable. With time, many of us realize that capability in a skill is a scale and not binary.

Think about a language that you do not speak even one word in. When put in an environment where everyone else is speaking that language, your world will suddenly become binary. There will be you, the person not capable of speaking that language, and everyone else that is.

Now think of yourself in an environment where people are being taught your native language. You will easily recognize varying levels of capability at speaking that language, the beginners, the novices, the more advanced, the teachers, and so on.

Thinking in binary terms in nature is discouraging, since the jump from incapable to capable can seem like an impossible task; whereas, perceiving capability in a skill as a scale with discrete steps makes reaching our potential a more achievable goal.

Truthfully, many of us continue to think in binary terms in regards to a sense of capability, something that can be quite emotionally draining and an obstacle to developing our skill sets.

The Success Diary exposes a child to a capability scale for a specific skill set. A child is capable at a skill to some extent and this capability can grow in discrete steps.

Take the example of being able to sit in class. When initially coming to the first grade, many children need to go from minimal expectations regarding sitting and concentrating, to sitting for about 45 minutes without getting up, during multiple sessions in a day.

From the child's perspective this transition may seem impossible, as it may be perceived as switching from relative freedom of movement to extended periods of self-control.

Children utilizing a Success Diary for this skill can be shown that they are capable of sitting for 45 minutes twice a day (during monitoring sessions). If they are capable of doing this then they probably can learn to extend the skill to three times a day, and then four times a day, and so on.

With the help of a Success Diary, children should gradually, with each experience of looking at The Success Diary, learn how capable they are at the defined skill set and how they are able to grow.

It is important to highlight that the goal of The Success Diary is not simply to be positive. It is a monitoring device meant to assist children in calculating their capability at a skill set (clinical psychologists may look at it as a transformational object assisting in self-reflection).

Just like any monitoring device, we want it to be as accurate as possible. This means that it is crucial that positive "marks" are given only when deserved. This is elaborated on in Chapter 7.

The Success Diary is a Measure of Capability

The Success Diary can be seen as a material measuring device to assist children in gauging their capability. Week by week, they are able to see how capable they are in the defined skill set. Upon seeing their weekly achievements, they may try to improve on themselves, testing their potential.

This is where we can actually learn from them. The energy to grow, inherently present in children, is something for us adults to emulate and rekindle in ourselves.

You will notice that an integral part of The Success Diary is that a child cannot fail. This is because, unlike with many other behavior modification techniques, there are no negative marks. Think of it like a scale. You cannot have negative weight, can you?

Even just one instance of practicing a defined skill set per week is a success, a measurement of capability, a starting point for growth.

Managing to climb a 10-foot wall, even once, proves to me that I can!

A child that does not gain many successes in a week may get discouraged, but hopefully this will push him/her to try harder in the future.

It is crucial that you, the teacher, and the parents consistently remind the child that he/she cannot fail. The Success Diary is not a test. The child needs to be reminded that it is just to show him/her how capable he/she is.

Motivating a Child for Success

Our job is to keep the child focused on capabilities, providing motivation when the need arises. Even if a child rips the diary up, that is just an opportunity to discuss frustrations and try again. If the child destroyed the book after three weeks then next time you can try go for four weeks. Remember, the focus is Success, not as a vision in the future but actual Success at its current level, doubled with encouragement to elevate that level (some of the specifics are elaborated on in Chapter 7).

For example, in the case of Michael, when he started using his Success Diary, we told him that we want to show him that he can be a nice guy without resorting to violence. We made it clear to him from the beginning that we believed he could do it.

Of no less importance, we did not waiver in our confidence that he could change. We gave him a consistent signal that he could be a nice guy, even when he continued fighting.

After one month, the whole collaborative triangle met and reviewed his Success Diary. Michael's book was crumpled and unadorned. He did not put much faith into the technique.

He clearly did not think himself capable.

We emphasized the sessions that he did help others without resorting to violence. I flipped through his book and stated, "Do you see that you are capable?"

He started arguing with me that he still had had many fights during the month, but I persisted in saying that he had proven he was capable of being a nice guy without fighting.

His teacher further pointed out that the frequency of fighting had decreased during monitoring sessions.

Michael began to see that he was managing to practice his new skill set, which was our goal. In other words, we redirected him towards the fact that he was capable of success.

Michael started to take ownership of his Success Diary. Evidence of this was seen in how he now treated the book. Suddenly, there were stickers of his favorite sports team plastered all over the spare pages and on the cover.

For the rest of the implementation of The Success Diary, Michael did not have a single physical altercation.

He had even been observed teaching his younger brother how to be good without fighting.

This was the point where theory became reality. It was evident that Michael had begun to believe that he was capable of change.

It is important to note that if we had not believed in his potential abilities and communicated this conviction to him unwaveringly, the intervention would probably not have worked.

We are requesting a leap of faith. If we ourselves do not trust in a child's ability to grow, then how can we expect the child to believe? Children are very good at reading us.

Children Require Opportunities to Practice the New Skill

Another aspect of communicating trust to the child is being able to periodically take a step back and let him/her figure things out for himself/herself. This means that even if we see that children are about to make a mistake, we should not always intervene (unless of course they are putting their own or someone else's life/health at risk).

This is especially important during the monitoring sessions. Let them make mistakes. Trial and error, with follow up discussions is a natural and effective way of learning.

Think of learning a new skill set in terms of education practices. We know now that learning is more efficient when a person gets the opportunity to answer a question, even if they make a mistake.

For example, if I want to teach children to write a word, I could either show them how the word is spelled (asking them to memorize it) or I could ask them to first try to spell it themselves (correcting them if they make an error). The latter method is more effective since we are allowed the time to process and attempt a solution of our own.

I believe that the same logic applies to most forms of learning, including behavioral skill sets. Let the child make a mistake and then after that have a conversation with them, asking them where they made a good decision and where they can improve.

Children that are allowed to make errors feel empowered. They feel trusted by a parent or a teacher. As stated above, this is important because trust is a two way street. The same way we want children to trust our word, we want them to perceive our trust in them.

Homework for the Teacher

1. From a scale of one to ten how capable do you think you are in the following actions: talking to resistant parents, writing essays, checking homework, baking cupcakes, doing your taxes?
2. From a scale of one to ten rate three children in your class in their abilities to plan for a typical school day.

7

Changing the Dysfunctional Behavior

Monitor for Success

So, working in a collaborative triangle, the appropriate steps have been taken, culminating in a Success Diary. You (teacher and parents) are going to provide the child with a guided opportunity for growth with the explicit message that an effort to change is expected. Moving forward, the goal is to monitor for success levels while maintaining an encouraging environment. The all-embracing message is, "We know you are capable of success and now it is your turn to show us how capable you are."

Before moving forward, just one side note. In general, as much as it is feasible, any discussions regarding a Success Diary should be held in private. In my experience, embarrassment can be an antecedent to non-compliance with any therapeutic plan.

Step One: Initiate The Success Diary

The day the monitoring begins should be commemorated in a sincere, positive ceremony (optionally even with cake) where the importance of the child's Success Diary is reinforced.

Remember that a large part of the team's job is to keep a child motivated. In turn, this communicates to the child that his/her personal growth is of great importance.

The initiation of the monitoring period should never be punitive. Just by being given a Success Diary, the child is already receiving signals that he or she needs to change (as well as during the steps towards its development). Although necessary, this message can feel aversive.

Basically, having the intervention implemented is in itself a negative consequence; it is a wake-up call.

Imagine if you received a work improvement plan at your job. No matter how positive the presentation, the bottom line is clear; something you are doing is not satisfactory and you need to improve.

In other words, at this stage you can sugarcoat the intervention as long as you remind the child the reason for the intervention. This does not have to take a long time but it is a crucial step.

This is also the stage to try to gauge the child's level of comprehension of the intervention. Allow him/her space to ask questions and clarify anything that you feel was not fully understood.

Step Two: Monitor According to the Schedule

During the implementation period of The Success Diary, you, the teacher, are responsible for the monitoring. This is mainly about measuring behavior during the scheduled sessions, and only during these sessions.

Perform observations during the predefined monitoring sessions and at the end of a session request that the child bring you his/her Success Diary. For younger children if you feel it necessary, remind them prior to the sessions that they are going to be monitored. Older children should generally be able to remember by themselves.

Some children prefer that during the day The Success Diary be in your possession. This is okay as long that it is clear whom it belongs to.

It is important that you focus only on the scheduled sessions and solely on the defined skill set. Even if the child presented with a dysfunctional behavior five minutes prior to the lesson, The Success Diary only measures his/her behavior during that lesson.

If the child presents with dysfunctional behaviors, unrelated to The Success Diary, at any time during the day, including during the monitoring sessions, then do whatever you normally would do.

The Success Diary is a supplementary tool and does not replace your own techniques.

If the dysfunctional behavior that is being focused on occurs then react the way you usually would. For example, if Angela would steal candy, during the monitoring sessions or at any time during the day, she would still be sent to the principal's office.

Step Three: Recognize the Successful Practice of a Skill Set

Marking down the children's progress is simple enough. If they practiced one of their skills during the session, draw a smiley (or a plus sign for older children) in the appropriate place in the monitoring table, under the corresponding cell for that time and referenced skill.

Even if they did not get a smiley (i.e. they did not practice this skill successfully) ensure to put your initial every time you review The Success Diary. This way the whole team can see that you are monitoring.

It is at your discretion as the teacher to determine when the child has had a success.

The rule of thumb is balance; do not be too harsh or too easy going. If the child clearly made an effort, then they get a smiley. For example, if Michael was polite to his teacher during a monitored lesson (e.g. keeping a calm tone and refraining from being argumentative) then he got a positive mark.

Angela preferred getting strawberry stickers over smileys. If she was seen making a healthy choice during snack time then she got a strawberry sticker for that skill. If she further shared her snack then she would get another sticker for that session.

Many teachers find out that a child needs to go at a slower pace than they initially thought. This is when you uncover evidence that the child really does need to learn the chosen skill.

If during the monitored session children present with the dysfunctional behavior related to that skill, then no matter what effort they made, they do not earn a smiley. This is due to the fact that they did not succeed in utilizing the skill that is meant to replace the dysfunctional behavior.

Make sure that in this scenario you are not communicating punishment. No frowns in this book. Remember, this is a measure of capability. The idea is to encourage the child to try harder to practice their skill set.

Think of yourself as the first mate and the child, the captain. You are the captain's confidant, providing feedback on which direction to steer the ship. The direction? A self-sustaining change where the child has acquired a higher level of capability in the chosen skill set.

Also, if, for example, the skill set is to improve social behaviors and the child suddenly does not do his/her homework, it should be remembered that this Success Diary is not related to homework.

Younger children may even need reminders about the scope, as they sometimes will assume that their Success Diaries cover all dysfunctional behaviors.

Step Four: Continue to Motivate throughout the Intervention

You can utilize The Success Diary as a motivational tool at any point in the day. If, during a period when not being monitored, a child presents with the dysfunctional behavior that we are trying to get him/her to replace, you can review his/her Success Diary together. This is a way to reaffirm that you believe that the child is capable of succeeding. Just make sure that it is understood that that instance of behavior is not recorded in the diary.

Regardless of these scenarios, The Success Diary should be reviewed together on a weekly basis. Flip back through the pages and celebrate successes. If a child feels incapable, redirect attention to the level of success. Express the words "can" and "capable" often.

This weekly review is one of the most important steps in the intervention and should be done with a lot of positive energy. In many cases, I have seen a child's eyes light up at the reminder of so many weeks of examples of success. Refer to Concept Box 7.1 for a discussion on the power of material tools.

CONCEPT BOX #7.1

Material Psychology

To illustrate the concept of Material Psychology it would be best to recount a personal story. When I was 13 years old I purchased my first bicycle from my mother's boyfriend. It was a cruiser bike, white with the word Peugeot inscribed on the middle bar. It was just a bicycle, but to me it was so much more.

My two best friends were suddenly geographically in my reach. This afforded us the opportunity to go on a myriad of adventures, some fun and some scary, but all invigorating experiences of emotional and social development.

This oversized hunk of metal and rubber transcended into an extension of who I was. A curious but painfully introspective child was suddenly provided the opportunity to ride off on adventures, to investigate the world, and further explore his mind. It was now in my power not to be lonely anymore.

Even the fact that I had purchased the bicycle from my mother's boyfriend had meant something to me. He was a father figure. Teaching me another treasured lesson; the value of a material item increases when it comes with a price.

As I glimpse into the many memories afforded me by this bicycle, I recall one late afternoon riding home through a giant field, made golden by the dry, tall grass. The trail I was ambling through was well trodden, worn down to a smooth winding lane, light brown and sandy.

My mind faded into that mystical stream of consciousness where imagination, untethered, romps around in the field of creation.

In other words, I began to daydream, pondering as to how this specific through-way had been made. The small nuanced twists and turns suggested that no one person had drafted the layout of this path. No, this pattern, this blueprint, was the design of a group of random people, a social phenomenon.

As I pushed through this golden field, mind drifting, once or twice falling off my bicycle, I devised a plan of how I would make a hypothesis. This analytical expedition was one of my first sincere forays into the scientific method. More importantly, moments like this are fond memories that remind me of who I am.

As you can see, items are often more than just the materials that they are made from. This is true from the moment that they begin to fulfill a function.

As humans we are born with a predisposition to make and utilize tools, physical/conceptual objects that are branded with a goal in mind. Our evolution is often depicted by the advancement of the tools that we have devised through the millennia.

The multifaceted functions of a tool can be predefined and general, or specific to an individual. A bicycle facilitates the generic task of mode of transportation and sport; however, as you can see, subjectively it was a device that enabled me a journey of social, emotional, and intellectual learning.

I coined the term Material Psychology as a way to describe a plethora of existing methods that conceptualize internal psychological dilemmas and solutions through the use of physical tools. These therapeutic approaches leverage our natural tendencies to inject personality and meaning into the tools that we use.

Personalized objects, like The Success Diary, act as proxy to personal development by reflecting to us aspects of our personality, allowing us opportunities to review who we are and how we need to grow. It is like looking in a mirror and seeing a reflection of your soul; then noticing that you have a piece of spinach stuck between two of your ethereal teeth.

Can you think of any treasured items from your own childhood that fulfilled functions above and beyond the intended purpose? A blanky that made you feel safe? A hat that transformed you into an adventurer? A pen that made you into a poet?

Now think about the tools of your trade. It is in the little details that we can perceive how an item means more to us individually than to an onlooker. These are the moments when an object elicits a complex emotion, hard to describe to anyone that has not experienced something similar. Is it in the smell of a new set of crayons? Is it in the crinkle of festive wrapping paper? Is it in the sight of a well-organized desk?

As you go through the intervention with a child, try and notice if there are any hints that suggest that the physical diary is more than just a book with writing and stickers on it. This is a sure way of recognizing if ownership of the material tool has occurred. I personally have noticed a positive reaction in many children that hear the rustling of the pages as a teacher flips back through his/her Success Diary, recognizing all of the successful sessions.

Depending on the availability and motivation of the parents, as well as your own schedule, have a collaborative triangle meeting at least three times during the monitoring period. At a minimum, try to have a weekly phone conversation with the parents to ensure that they are also reviewing The Success Diary with their child.

Many teachers that I have worked with would encourage the parents to give weekly prizes for a child if he/she actively participated in the intervention. This was measured by children having their books with them at all monitoring sessions, sharing their books with their parents, and making an effort to personalize their Success Diaries.

Some parents would bring the child a present on the day that The Success Diary was initiated and on the day it ended. The idea is to reward a child for bonding with their Success Diary. This is fine; however, do not reward a child for successfully utilizing a skill set during a monitoring session (other than putting a smiley in the table). See Concept Box 7.2 for a discussion on reinforcement.

CONCEPT BOX #7.2

Reinforcing a Learning Experience

Most behavior modification charts and applied behavior analysis techniques incorporate an element of rewards, such as praise, candy, money, or tokens towards larger prizes. The theory is that we are consistently reinforcing the functional behaviors. The Success Diary works similarly; however, what is being reinforced is exposure to an experience.

Both approaches are founded on theories of learning that incorporate manifold discreet instances of reinforcement, the difference being the scope of that reinforcement. In a way, behavior modification charts are a form of behavioral micromanaging, focusing on specific behaviors as they occur. They can be very effective but in my eyes at times overbearing.

The Success Diary, on the other hand, reinforces an effort at becoming more capable at a skill. That is, you are primarily rewarding utilization of The Success Diary, regardless of level of success. The consistent reinforcement is the encouragement and attention provided by you and the parents.

I personally prefer that a Success Diary intervention utilize verbal praise alone. In my experience most children will respond to attention. With that said, some children will come to the intervention with an expectation that they be rewarded with tangibles, for good behavior. This is often due to previous exposure to behavior improvement plans and home education.

In the case of The Success Diary, tangible rewards can be given for participation but not for success level. In other words, no matter how little success there is, the child gets a prize for continuing to utilize his/her Success Diary (e.g. a present once a week, as long as the diary was presented in all monitoring sessions). On the other hand, level of success during each monitoring session is more correctly considered a measurement and not a reward.

Remember, this intervention is about personal development. A child motivated to pursue a journey of social and emotional learning is evidently ready to go through a self-sustaining transformation. This state of mind is what we want to reinforce, an accomplishment that in many ways, is of higher import than the final level of success achieved.

Step Five: Prepare the Child for the End of the Intervention

During the last four weeks of the intervention on every Monday, inform the child how many weeks he or she has left. On varying levels, this is a very powerful intervention for children. They need to be reminded how much time is left so that they do not feel suddenly abandoned when it ends.

Furthermore, some children, especially ones that feel the need to have control, may begin with an oppositional attitude. They will not take part initially but have the intention of taking part in the end. Reminding them when the end is coming assists them in waking up in time.

Step Six: At the End Celebrate Success

When the intervention has finished, the closing meeting should be treated with the same reverence as when the monitoring began. This is a time to recognize success, any level of success. Most children at this point will have had some change in behavior. If possible, have the parents present for this part.

Review the whole intervention from beginning to end, starting with the reason why they needed a Success Diary, through any milestones achieved, obstacles overcome, and ending in a celebration of their success.

Take it slowly and make it personal. A child's perspective of time is different from ours.

Sixteen weeks is a long adventurous journey.

Even if there still was no change in dysfunctional behavior, the review is still of great importance, since this does not mean that a child did not learn anything. We want the child to have a positive experience to reflect on at a later time.

Some children take longer to make changes.

The therapeutic experience of using a Success Diary leaves a mark on the mind, and we hope that the change occurs in a timely fashion. This, however, is not always the case.

In the end, the change is up to the child. Some learn in jumps, and others slow and steady. Some prefer to be guided, whereas others prefer to maintain a sense of control, saving learning moments for when they believe that no one is looking.

Step Seven: Set Up a Follow-up Meeting

If possible, I recommend that the collaborative triangle schedule a follow-up meeting about one or two months later. As mentioned, our goal is to realize a sustainable change. Some children will adopt positive behavior during the intervention but immediately regress once they are not being monitored anymore.

The purpose of this follow-up meeting is to reaffirm three things to the child. The first is that he/she is still in the same positive environment. The support team wants to convey that they are still there, working together, that the collaborative triangle is still intact.

The second is to reiterate the belief that the child is capable. We want this thought to linger, and a reminder from time to time is very important, since otherwise the child may regress to his/her previous habits.

The third is a clear signal to the child that, even though the intervention is over, the expectations are still there. He/she cannot continue to present with dysfunctional behaviors.

Step Eight: Stepping Back

In summation, a collaborative triangle has been formed, the problem has been named, a skill set has been defined, and a Success Diary has been made and implemented. All of these stages were taken while involving the child in as many steps of planning as possible.

Now the hard part begins.

The support system (i.e. you and the parents) needs to take a step back. Not to totally step away but yes to allow children some freedom to test out what they have learned.

Only after the monitoring sessions have ended does the most crucial part of learning occur. The child must carry on developing his/her capability in a skill despite not getting that systematic positive feedback/attention that he/she may have gotten used to.

At this point the feedback should mainly be coming from within.

The child should actively be attempting to use the learned skill. This is a sure test that someone has gone through a self-sustaining transformation.

In other words, go back to giving the children the same amount of attention you would give to any child. Let them figure things out for themselves and intervene only when a reminder of capability is necessarily required.

For example, if Michael had begun fighting again on a daily basis, the team would have met up together and gone through his Success Diary, refocusing him on how capable he had proven himself. For this reason it is best to preserve the child's Success Diary after the intervention has ended.

It is a treasured object that embodies a child's capability to grow.

Often children will keep their diaries and refer to them from time to time without any prompting from you or their parents. This too is a sign of a child at least attempting to achieve a self-sustaining change.

Injecting Your Personality into the Intervention

As this guide comes to an end, I wanted to digress to the beginning. This book's focus is injecting personality into behavior modification. I highlighted the personality of the children that require such an intervention, their needs, their desires, their creative flairs, their dysfunctional behaviors, and their ability to grow.

What I did not elaborate on enough is your personality.

This may be one of the biggest advantages of not leaning solely on behavioral methods. Your personality is important. In fact it is crucial.

I hope that it has been clear in the pages of this handbook the extent to which you have an effect on children's social and emotional development. Use your creativity, and trust your intuition.

On a final note, a word of encouragement for you, the teacher. The main reason I chose to write this book for teachers and not for other professionals in the field was to show my gratitude for what you do.

You may not have a Success Diary of your own but you have years and years of putting in the time to educate our children. I hope that you can visualize those many days and all of the little faces as you flip back through your "diary."

In other words, you are capable. Thank you!

Thank you not just for what you do but also for who you are.

Homework for the Teacher

1. Do something fun.

For Product Safety Concerns and Information please contact our EU representative GPSR@taylorandfrancis.com
Taylor & Francis Verlag GmbH, Kaufingerstraße 24, 80331 München, Germany

www.ingramcontent.com/pod-product-compliance
Lightning Source LLC
Chambersburg PA
CBHW061845300426
44115CB00013B/2515